Restored from the Ashes of a Broken Life

A True Story of Addiction, Recovery, Redemption, and Faith

by Loren E. McWilliams, Sr.

For Passion Publishing, LLC
Bellingham, WA

FOR-PASSION
PUBLISHING

Published by For Passion Publishing Company, LLC

Bellingham WA 98226 U.S.A.

www.ForPassionPublishing.com

First Edition.

Printed in the United States of America.

Dedication

I dedicate this book to those who stuck with me and, with the help of Jesus Christ, prayed for me: my partner, children and grandchildren, my parents, and the rest of my beautiful family. You showed me that life is precious and worth living.

Bible Verses

The bible verses on these pages come from the
New International Reader's Version (NirV).

Affirmations

The appendix contains over 200 affirmations that have helped me with recovery or touched my life in a meaningful way.

I hope you will refer to them as you read this book, and when you finish it. May you find solace and inspiration in those words.

- Loren

RON PHILLIS
I THANK GOD
EACH TIME I
THINK OF YOU

GOD BLESS
YOU KEEP YOU
LOREN M.
3-2022

A Note from the Author

The stories in this book are true. I have changed some of the names to honor their privacy.

Although I am sharing stories of drug and alcohol abuse, I in no way want to glorify the destructive lifestyle of addiction. If you need help, please get in touch with one of the many organizations that can help with your recovery. I have listed a few below, but there are many others.

> **Alcoholics Anonymous (AA)** - An international fellowship of men and women who have had a drinking problem. The organization is nonprofessional, self-supporting, multiracial, apolitical, and has chapters throughout the world. Membership is open to anyone who wants to do something about their drinking problem. Website: aa.org

> **Narcotics Anonymous (NA)** – Similar to AA but aimed at people with addictions to hardcore drugs. Website: na.org

> **The Most Excellent Way** - A worldwide ministry dedicated to recovery. If you want your recovery deeply steeped in the teachings of Jesus, this could be the way to go. Website: tmewcf.org

> **Celebrate Recovery** - A Christ-centered, 12-Step recovery program for anyone struggling with hurt, pain, or addiction of any kind. Website: celebraterecovery.com

Table of Contents

Table of Contents

Introduction

"You can choose either blessings or curses."
- Deuteronomy 30:19

Until I found Jesus, I chose curses. Like many who walk among us, and perhaps even you, I lived in fear, hopelessness, and despair. I destroyed my life with poor choices and became angry at God. If you are mad at God now, then this book is for you. If a loved one is in a dark place, this book is for you, too. If you are in that dark place, imagine that this book is holding your hand – that I am holding your hand, or perhaps God is. I also wrote this book to inspire anyone who chooses to read it.

If you don't believe in God or doubt God, I get it. I have been in that place, wallowed in self-pity, addiction, anger, and despair. With God's help, I made it through.

This is the story I want to tell.

I want to shout my story from the mountaintops, but this book will have to suffice.

My life was broken by the bondage of drugs, alcohol, and many other obsessive and compulsive behaviors. Out of the ashes of that broken life, I found redemption.

I am unapologetically a Christian, a man of God, a sinner saved by grace.

Where once I chose curses, I now choose the blessings.

Chapter 1

The Farm

"Then we will no longer be infants, tossed back and forth by the waves, and blown here and there by every wind of teaching and by the cunning and craftiness of people in their deceitful scheming."
Ephesians 4:14

I grew up in Custer, a small quiet town in rural northwest Washington just a few miles from the Canadian border. Along Main Street stood a gas station, a church, a tavern, and the Custer Country Store where many of the 100 or so residents held charge accounts. My parents settled there in the late 1950s, as did country singer Loretta Lynn. Mrs. Lynn and her husband, Oliver "Doolittle" Lynn, are likely the only reason anyone outside Custer has ever heard of the town. Nothing much happened there.

My family lived the simplicity of country folk. Typical of life in small-town rural America, we never locked our doors and the air often smelled like manure, which one got used to.

My uncle, parents, four siblings, and I lived on a small 40-acre ranch where we raised Black Angus beef. I was the youngest of the brood. My mother was 40, and my father was 50 when I came into the world.

A creek ran through the middle of our property, bringing pure fresh water from the foothills. Beyond the foothills loomed the rugged snow-capped Cascades to the east, and the B.C. Coastal Range to the north. Mount Baker, a sleeping giant of a volcano, watched over the valley. Sometimes we packed mud to dam the creek so we could have a swimming hole.

Growing up with cattle, I always had my favorite. One was a bull we named Bart. I loved that bull - he was my buddy! I often went to the barn just to hang with him. He was massive but was gentle with a mellow disposition. I even tried to ride him a couple of times.

The neighbor kids would join us to play outside. We might make a hay fort, play football, or any other sport or game we could think of. I enjoyed football as a kid and still do to this day, although it was tough for me to play due to a disability.

I was pigeon-toed as a small child and didn't walk until I was two years old. Children teased and ridiculed the way I walked. They called me "crippled bow-legged". I felt insecure and inadequate, especially in gym class. I could not run. When it came time to climb the rope, a popular activity in PE in those days, I couldn't make it to the first knot.

I knew something was wrong with me, but I didn't know exactly what. At eight years old, I was diagnosed with an inherited disorder that I would not comprehend until much later. It was called Charcot-Marie-Tooth Disease, so when I heard the diagnosis, I assumed it related to my teeth, not my legs.

Despite my disability, I had a relatively happy childhood. I knew I was loved.

My father suffered from mental health issues and was absent much of the time. When he was young, he was bucked off a horse and landed on his spine on a cement slab. While I was still a small child, he had a nervous breakdown. He was admitted to a mental health hospital in Sedro Wooley, a town about 40 miles away at the foot of the Cascade Mountains. They gave him electric shock treatment and prescribed Thorazine. Upon his return to the farm, he was never the same person.

As a result of his mental condition, he was absent much of the time and lacked motivation. For these reasons, I have few memories of him before my teenage years. We didn't do the "normal" father-son activities like playing catch or going hunting.

As the youngest child, my mother spoiled me a bit – at least, that is what my siblings like to tell me. There is probably some truth to that. My mother did her best to instill good morals in all of us.

I did well in school and generally got good grades. Reading and writing were strong points. I struggled with math.

We regularly attended the Zion Lutheran Church. The church building was a formidable structure for such a small town. Its bright white exterior stood out among the lush green fields and forests that surrounded it. Love of God and fellow man was woven into our lives at home and church, which gave me a solid foundation of good morals and values. I always felt God loved me and continue to feel that way to this day.

Unfortunately, as was common with most people in those days, especially with men, I learned to hide my feelings behind a stoic face and internalize frustration, anger, and other intense emotions when they arose.

We did not travel outside of Custer very often. Occasionally we'd make the short drive to the seaside town of Birch Bay or take longer car trips to the Washington coast. We sometimes visited an aunt and uncle who lived in Pendleton, Oregon, where we would tube down a river near their house. A few times, we attended the Pendleton Round-Up, a top-notch rodeo. Once, we drove to Bakersfield, California, to attend my sister's wedding.

I began to shed the innocence of my young, sheltered life in Custer when my family moved us to the neighboring town of Ferndale the summer of my eighth-grade year. Although still a relatively small town, Ferndale had many times the population of Custer. Change has always been difficult for me, a dynamic that continues to this day. Moving from the house that had anchored my childhood catapulted me from a zone of comfort and predictability I had taken for granted. A cloud of insecurity loomed over me, foreshadowing the changes that were about to alter the trajectory of my life.

After my parents sold their farm, they shipped the cattle back to my uncle's farm in Missouri. Shortly after, my mom, dad, brother, and I visited my father's family there. I was excited to see Bart the bull again. We crossed the country in a 1963 Chevy Corvair. Since we didn't travel much, it was the trip of a lifetime for me. Some of the most vivid memories of my childhood are from that trip.

Even growing up in the shadow of the rugged North Cascades, the majesty of the Rocky Mountains took my breath away.

After crossing the Rockies, something that sticks in my mind was my first experience with "real" thunderstorms. Lightning is rare in western Washington state where the storms may blow hard and drop a lot of rain but lack the drama of big thunderstorms. I was in awe of the powerful thunderstorms that boomed across the Midwest.

Once, I was startled awake by the loudest bang I think I had ever heard. Lightning streaked across the night sky, followed by earth-shaking thundercracks. It felt as if the world itself was coming to an end. I felt terrified and crawled into my parent's bed for comfort. My father wasn't having any of it. He got mad for getting into his bed, called me a baby, and told me I needed to go back to my bed. My dad had grown up in Kansas and, unlike me, was accustomed to the crackling violence of thunderstorms. When we got up the next day, I was surprised that nobody even mentioned the storm. The sun was out, and everything was back to normal.

When we finally reached the farm where our former cattle now lived, I finally got to see my bull, Bart. He was an intelligent fellow and remembered me.

My uncle's ranch was much bigger than the one we had in Custer. He had upward of 600 acres, and legend has it he bought it from a relative of the notorious bank robber Pretty Boy Floyd. To give credence to the legend, several bullet-ridden 1930s era cars dotted the fields. My brother and I searched high and low for stolen loot but never found any.

We visited a cemetery where many of my paternal ancestors were buried. It was weird seeing my name on a tombstone. I was named after my grandfather, Loren Heckard. I was around three years old when he passed away, but I still had memories of him. To this day, I am struck by the fact that my grandparents were born in the 1800s.

It felt special to be with my parents on that trip, especially my father, as we had never been close. After this trip, my mother sat me down and explained my father's mental health issues and how they began after he fell off a horse. I didn't completely comprehend how the pieces fit together, but I accepted her words and moved on.

Upon returning home to Custer, stirring desires and compulsions began to pulse through my adolescent mind and body. Things were about to change in significant ways for me, and not for the better.

On the romantic side, I soon received my first kiss under the bleachers at Ferndale High School from the prettiest girl in school. Her name was Tonjha. She had moved to our town from Portland, Oregon, and often wore short dresses in 6th and 7th grade. All the boys were crazy for her, and to my surprise, she absolutely adored me. This, of course, made the other boys incredibly jealous. Our young, budding romance was short-lived as she soon moved away again.

Her departure left me sad and heartbroken. To that point in my life, she was the cutest girl I had ever laid eyes on. Our brief connection was the first stitch in a pattern that I would repeat for many years to come as my attraction to beautiful women would contribute to my demise.

The girls at school seemed to like my blue eyes, curly hair, and straight teeth. Although I felt self-conscious about it, they didn't seem to mind the way I walked.

Tonjha would be far from the first girl who broke my heart in those years. I even had one relationship where I was sure we would marry, have children, and spend the rest of our lives together.

Since Custer and Ferndale are so close, and the area at the time was relatively unpopulated, I already knew most of the kids I went to school with in Ferndale even before we moved. This helped tremendously during my freshman year. Although it took some getting used to, my transition to high school went relatively smoothly. For the most part, the kids at school were friendly. That said, it did not take long to figure out which kids I would be hanging out with.

I tried marijuana for the first time one Friday night after a football game. I liked how it made me feel, and I began to smoke pot regularly. As a result, I began affiliating with the "stoner" crowd at school.

Another school clique, the "jocks", would harass and bully me because of how I walked. They called me names like "bull legged" and "crippled". Sometimes this would lead to fights. It soon dawned on me that they were also insecure, and they picked on me and others to feel better about themselves. That made me feel a little better, but also sad. I knew some of those jocks since I grew up with a few of them in Custer. Some were nice to me because of our childhood history together, but most were cruel and picked on me.

The stoners were much kinder. They wanted to party and didn't care what kind of clothes you wore, if you played sports, how much money your parents made, or if you walked funny. Their focus was getting high, goofing off, and having fun.

From marijuana, I moved on to cigarettes. Smoking was an act of defiance against my parents and other authority figures. At first, it all seemed harmless. Little did I realize that these were the first steps of a substance abuse problem that would ultimately derail my life. For me, and contrary to what many pot smokers would say, marijuana was indeed a gateway drug. Although my pot-smoking started gradually, I was soon smoking as much of it as I could get my hands on.

I had a newspaper route at that time, which gave me the money to buy marijuana and party on weekends.

On Fridays in the fall, I would inevitably inform my parents I was going to the football game. My stoner friends and I would attend for a little while, then go off with whoever was up to party. At the parties, there was plenty of marijuana and beer. I soon became accustomed to the partying lifestyle. I began to drink heavily and smoke marijuana daily.

My friends and I would sometimes break into a house, often that of a girlfriend, to steal alcohol. That's usually all we stole, although if we noticed some nice stereo equipment or albums, we might take those, too. While most students in my high school focused on working towards college, their careers, and other dreams, I put my energy into where my next fix would come from.

These choices introduced me to a dark world of hopelessness, fear, guilt, and shame. It didn't take long to lead to some minor depression, excessive pain, and misery. More would soon follow.

My first arrest and incarceration happened when I was 15. I had taken my parents' car to pick up a small keg of beer. I got drunk and when I returned the car to my house, forgot to remove the keg. My father was furious and called the police. I didn't even have a driver's license yet. It was the first of many run-ins with the law. I thought my parents would bail me out, but they were steadfast in wanting me to learn the consequences of my poor choices. I spent two or three days in juvie.

I could tell my father was disappointed in me, and I suspect my mother was, too, although she didn't talk much about it. At the same time, my mother's unconditional love for me was always filled with grace and forgiveness. To this day, the way she loved me reminds me of how much our Lord and Savior shows His grace and forgiveness.

This was just one step of a vicious cycle that would lead to many jails, institutions, and near-death experiences. I only wanted to hang out with other kids who smoked weed, partied, and showed contempt for institutions, the law, and their own well-being.

Soon after my release from juvie, I traded my mini bike for a Ford Galaxie 500. It was an awful poorly-made well-used car. I continued to drive without a driver's license, and eventually, I was caught and cited for driving without a license. The police impounded the car. I asked my mom to loan me the money to get the car back, but she refused. That's how I lost my first car.

It was a normal thing for me to drive intoxicated during my high school years. I never received a DUI citation, but I deserved many – and it wasn't for lack of being caught by the cops. In those days, the police would just pull me over, dump out the beer, and tell me to go home and stay there. It's by the grace of God that I didn't die in a car crash, let alone kill or hurt someone else.

By the time I turned 17, I was an early-stage chronic alcoholic and drug addict. Doing drugs became my adopted lifestyle. My self-esteem was in the gutter.

I somehow managed to make it through high school with Cs and Ds, but I got kicked out of high school my senior year for getting in a fistfight with the vice principal. My parents were furious. I was leaving my boyhood behind in dramatic fashion and becoming an immature, irresponsible drug addict.

I would stay up all night and sleep in all day. My parents tried to get me to join the Navy. Unfortunately, due to my physical limitations, I was rejected. I wanted to join the Air Force, but no branch of the armed services would accept me.

Instead, my parents sent me to Navy Camp in Oak Harbor, Washington, about an hour and a half south of Ferndale. At Navy Camp you did the same things you would in the Navy – get up, do calisthenics, eat with the other sailors, but you weren't actually in the Navy, and you didn't fly in the jets.

Being the young rebel and addict, I smuggled in some marijuana. When I smoked it with another kid, we got caught and were hauled off to the brig. I got a lecture from the SP (Shore Police) Military about my behavior and was released. They wanted to scare me by telling me that I would go to jail for a long time if I continued this kind of behavior. I wish I had listened; they were 100% correct.

I smoked marijuana whether I was happy, sad, angry, or depressed. I used it to numb any feelings I had. I continued this toxic pattern throughout my years of active addiction.

In recovery, I learned that people stop growing mentally, emotionally, and spiritually at the age they pick up their first drug or drink. This stunting of growth continues until they become sober, and then the road to achieve "normal" maturity for one's age can take years or decades and sometimes never happens. Looking back, I can see how my addictions arrested my development into adulthood and stole a good part of my youth.

The chains of addiction are powerful. They are relentless, baffling, and cunning. I now believe that every time I faced a choice between good and bad or right and wrong, it was also a choice between serving God or serving the demons of addiction.

I would stand at the crossroads many times. One day, by divine guidance, I broke the chains of addiction.

With God's help, I was released from the bondage that had been inside me for so many years. I arose from the ashes of a broken life. On the other side, I found love, acceptance, and forgiveness.

That would come later. Much later.

Chapter 2

The Vessel

**"But we have this treasure in jars of clay
to show that this all-surpassing power
is from God and not from us."
2 Corinthians 4:7**

In Chapter One I mentioned my diagnosis with Charcot-Marie-Tooth Disease, or CMT. In this chapter, I'd like to elaborate.

At eight years old, I was much smaller than most boys my age. I was also weak and, as I mentioned, I walked funny. I couldn't climb and run or do the other things that other children enjoyed.

My doctor wanted to see what was amiss and had me undergo some lab tests. One of the tests was a biopsy of my calf muscle. When the lab results came back, the doctor informed my parents that I had CMT. I didn't understand much about it but later learned that the doctors who discovered it had the last names Charcot, Marie, and Tooth; thus, Charcot-Marie-Tooth disease. It is a distant relative to multiple sclerosis (MS) but does not affect your life expectancy.

CMT is a hereditary neuromuscular condition caused by mutations to the genes to the X chromosome. When my brain tells my muscles to move, CMT slows that connection, giving me sluggish reflexes. The functioning of my hands and fine motor skills are often problematic. CMT frequently creates cramping or locking up of my lower legs and arms. CMT even caused me to have structural deformities in my feet, including high arches. It also produces chronic fatigue. With age, CMT triggers muscle atrophy.

Over 250,000 people in the U.S. have CMT. There are several types of CMT. Symptoms can vary depending on the type and the individual. Many have much more severe symptoms than I do.

Disability was no stranger to my family. My father was born crippled with severe scoliosis. I also have scoliosis, but not as severe as my father's. Two of my sisters were also diagnosed with CMT; as a result, one now uses a walker, and the other is in a wheelchair.

I have a cousin named Leonard who also has CMT and could barely walk and was unable to use his hands. He had a positive attitude and showed God's mercy and love through his great sense of humor. There is no treatment for CMT, but some of its manifestations can be addressed through surgery. When I was 18, I had reconstructive surgery on my feet that entailed transferring ligaments and tendons. They also lengthened both of my Achilles heels. Since then, I have had over a dozen more surgeries to address the ravages of CMT.

To this day, even with all the medical interventions, I suffer from severe muscle cramps that can radiate through my entire body. Sometimes they are so excruciating all I can do is stop what I'm doing and quietly endure the agony, although I also want to scream from the pain. I get by with some mild medication but avoid suppressing the pain with strong narcotics.

With physical therapy, I have learned to do moderate physical activities. Being active also staves off decline later in life. My sisters avoided exercise and paid dearly for it. I believe that is why they have required a wheelchair and a walker. So far, I've only had to use a cane, which was a relatively recent adaptation. By staying active, I hope that I won't have to succumb to other mobility aids, but there are no guarantees.

If one has CMT, they have a 50% chance of passing it on to their children. Fortunately, neither of my children inherited it, although one of my sisters with CMT passed it on to her daughter and grandchildren. A doctor once told me that I should not have children because of the risk. I chose to have kids despite that recommendation. If my children had been born with CMT, I would have loved them no less. After all, I am grateful that I was brought into the world, and my mother loved me deeply.

I often wish I didn't have CMT. However, I was made in His image. I believe we are all broken. Everyone has limitations and challenges of some kind. They may be physical, mental, emotional, or circumstantial.

I learned how to live within my pain and physical limitations. Even with the muscle cramps, chronic pain, and fatigue, I have been able to have a normal, functional life. And for this, I feel blessed beyond measure and feel eternally grateful.

Living with CMT affects you emotionally, mentally, physically, and certainly spiritually if you allow it to. I learned long ago that if my brain and my heart are fully functional, the most important parts of who I am are not disabled. I have derived much of my strength to carry on and thrive from my Lord and Savior, Jesus Christ. He has given me the courage not to give up the fight. I know that with Him by my side, it can be a victorious day.

Of course, I have my ups and downs. There are days when I don't want to get out of bed. During the most difficult and painful times, I remember that with hope, faith, and courage, tomorrow can be better.

One of the scriptures that I apply throughout the day is **Philippians 4:13**, "I can do all things through Christ who gives me strength." And He does! I have asked Jesus to remove this thorn in my flesh. He has told me, as he told Paul the Apostle, "My grace is sufficient."

If I had to select one word to describe my life, I would choose "grace". I'm not perfect, and nor can we be in this life. We need God's grace to see our lives as God does, for God's grace is enough for every moment we have on earth.

For most of my life, I felt less than. I never thought I belonged, and I lacked self-esteem. Perhaps most of us think such thoughts, or have in the past. Today, with God by my side, I have much more self-confidence. I am more personable. When problems arise, I feel capable of handling them. I know I can persevere. When I want to give up, I remember that there is always work to be done for the Kingdom of God.

I find comfort in verses like **Philippians 3:13-14.** "Brothers and sisters, I do not consider myself yet to have taken hold of it. But one thing I do: Forgetting what is behind and straining toward what is ahead, I press on toward the goal to win the prize for which God has called me heavenward in Christ Jesus." My Victory is in Him and Him alone.

It was difficult when I noticed people laughing or pointing at me for my disability. It has taken a lot of effort to overcome the embarrassment and fear of failure. Through my faith, I have learned to live with vision and purpose. I discovered that it's not about how far you fall but how many times you get back up. CMT has impeded my physical activities, but it has not dampened my spirit. Today I am blessed to have a loving family. I am grateful to be physically and emotionally close to my children and grandchildren. These wonderful people have supported me in my darkest hours. It is with God's grace and their help that I have been able to get back up.

I sometimes need to ask for help with physical tasks, and my family is always there for me. Other times, I need emotional support and I will call family members or close friends for help. I am grateful for this support network. On a daily basis, they encourage me to do what I can for myself and remind me not to push too hard.

A physical therapist told me that his wife, who had MS, rated her energy level with imaginary spoons. She saw her daily energy limit as a set of seven spoons. It might take her two spoons to get dressed and have breakfast, leaving her with five spoons for the day. Lunch might take another spoon, and going to the doctor would take another two, leaving her with one spoon for dinner and one more to be ready for bed. Since I am an avid pie connoisseur, I use the allotment of ten pieces of pie to get through the day. This has been another strategy to help me see CMT not as a problem but simply as another aspect of who I am.

I used to be too shy to talk about CMT, especially with friends and family. I felt angry, bitter, and ashamed. For most of my life, my diagnosis was the elephant in the room. Now I know that CMT is one small part of my story, and it doesn't define me. God gives me the courage to share my experiences with my disability, even in public.

God reminds me that every person walking the Earth truly has their challenges, whether visible or not. It just so happens that mine are more visible than most. With my first-hand experience of living with and overcoming many of the limitations of CMT, I have been able to offer help to others with significant challenges in their lives. Also, by expressing my feelings about living with CMT, God has made room in my life for better things: faith, family, friends, and fun. These four priorities are now my mantra.

I'm in my sixties now, and fatigue from CMT is probably the biggest challenge. I also suffer from arthritis, especially in my hands, back, and feet.

I pray that modern medicine may find better treatments for CMT, or perhaps even a cure. Until that day, people like me who suffer from CMT will need to rely on the understandings we have now and God's power to help us through. He has already shown me what I can do with CMT, even as others have told me I could not do those things.

Suffering from CMT, I've often felt the odds were stacked against me. I know that it's easy to trust God when things go our way but much harder when He puts obstacles in the way. I remind myself that He and He alone is the source of my strength, regardless if the odds are in my favor or not. There are seasons in life, but my relationship with God has always been there. Money, success, and even friends have come and gone. Yet throughout the physical challenges of CMT, I can stay focused on the Lord and continue to be in awe of the things He does in my life. Since I felt insecure most of my youth, I drifted away from God's design for my life. I scoffed at His plan and replaced it with my agenda. Today, as a man of God, I run to the Father, not from Him. I know that God holds me in the palm of his hand, and my future is bright and wonderful in Him.

It helps to remember that God does not want to harm you. **Jeremiah 29:11**: "' I know the plans I have for you,' announces the Lord. 'I want you to enjoy success. I do not plan to harm you. I will give you hope for the years to come.'"

There is nothing to be ashamed of in getting on your knees and committing your life to Christ. It is between you and God My greatest hope for readers of this book is that they realize anyone, regardless of disability, hardship, or challenge, can build a life worth living one day at a time in Jesus Christ.

"Dear Jesus, I know that I am a sinner. I know that you love me and want to save me, Jesus. I know that you are the Son of God who died on the cross for my sins. I believe God raised you from the dead. I now repent of my sins, and by faith, I receive you as Lord and Savior. Come into my heart, Jesus. Forgive me of my sins in the presence of the Holy Spirit. Come into my heart and save me. It's in your Name I pray. Amen."

Welcome, my friend. You are now a Christian, and your sins are forgiven. You now have the gift of eternal life in him.

Chapter 3

Tore Back

**"If you don't heal what hurt you,
you will bleed on people who didn't cut you."
Author unknown.**

Hurt people often hurt other people.

At the young age of 14, I began smoking cigarettes and marijuana, drinking alcohol, and having sex with girls. These were the unhealthy and destructive ways I attempted to feel in control of my life and deal with my disability. Instead, I was losing control and becoming an addict.

My first job delivering newspapers gave me the financial means to support the party lifestyle. I did my route seven days a week, covering the stores and residences in downtown Ferndale. I bought cigarettes out of a vending machine along my route for $0.35 a pack.

Between my low self-worth, anger toward God and growing addictions, I destroyed my life with poor choices. I was fired from my paper route when a kid called me a cripple. In a fit of anger and rage, I kicked him in the head.

Among the partying crowd I was well-liked, but in other circles there was mutual animosity. Even though I didn't like myself, girls did, even many who were not partiers. Many were one-night stands, but at least eight became short-term girlfriends. Dating came easy for me, but it might be more accurate to say that unhealthy relationships did. I became an expert in those. Between my lack of self-esteem, poor life skills, alcohol consumption, and drug use, I did not have what it took to nurture a romantic relationship and give it true meaning.

Although my mother taught me good morals and values, I ignored them. Sex, drugs, alcohol, rock and roll, and parties were my priorities. School and social activities outside of partying fell by the wayside. With the money I had made over time on my paper route, I purchased model cars, toys, and even a motorcycle. I traded or sold everything I could to buy cigarettes and intoxicants.

I now know that habitual sin, be it in the form of drugs, alcohol, or other compulsive behaviors, is a direct result of not having a relationship with Jesus Christ. In one way or another, at some point in our lives, we all turn our back on the One who can help us the most.

Proverbs 3: 5-6: "Trust in the Lord with all your heart. Do not depend on your understanding. In all your ways obey him. Then he will make your paths smooth and straight."

The path I followed through my youth was rough and tangled.

The path was also dark. What started as occasionally smoking or drinking became a daily routine. Everyone I associated with was on a similar track.

Drugs can easily sway a directionless life. First, a person takes the drug, and then the drug takes the person. One doesn't realize that when they start doing drugs, they are simultaneously selling their soul to the demons of addiction. The result is that one becomes a shell of their true selves. It can easily take everything anyone ever wanted or had. It robs your dreams and the very reasons you want to get out of bed in the morning.

Addiction has no limits to what it can and will destroy. Looking back over my life, the series of decisions I made put my life on a trajectory that could only lead to suffering, toxicity, and pushing God away. Drugs and alcohol are masters of deception. When I started using them, I thought they were the good things in life. They tricked me into thinking they would help me deal with my shame, isolation, and lack of self-worth. With a sleight of hand, they threw me deeper and deeper into the abyss.

"Tore back" is a slang expression for being so messed up, usually because of consuming drugs or alcohol, that one cannot properly function in society. Tore back was my motto for most of my young and adult life.

When multiple people tell you the same thing, it's wise to consider their counsel. So many people around me told me I had an addiction that I needed to confront. They included my siblings, children, other family members, and close friends. Not everyone around me was an enabler – some wanted to help me out of the darkness, but I ignored them and suffered for it. A friend who was a pastor told me that I would die if I didn't do something. Fortunately, my addictions didn't kill me, but they did put me in a downward spiral where I lost my business, my home, and many meaningful friendships. At one point I was homeless, living in a car with my girlfriend after I lost my apartment because I used my money to buy drugs and alcohol rather than pay the rent on my apartment.

When I was a teenager, you could buy a bag of marijuana for cheap – maybe around $10. It did not have the high THC levels that today's marijuana does, but it was smokeable, and it would get you high.

When I was around 14, some friends and I met some carnies who were in town working the Ferndale Pioneer Days festival. We cruised around with them through downtown Ferndale that night, and they decided they wanted to score some marijuana. I told them how to get to the house of my brother's friend, where I knew I could buy some. They gave me a $10 bill, and I went in and bought a bag, and I jumped back in the car. When we headed back through town, a police officer pulled us over for failing to use a turn signal – not surprising because we had all just smoked a couple of joints, including the driver.

The carnie I had handed the marijuana to had put it in his front shirt pocket, where it was visible to anyone who looked at him. It didn't occur to him to pull it out of his pocket when the cop came up to the car window. The cop noticed it immediately and asked him to exit the car. Ferndale was a relatively small town back then, and everyone knew everyone. The officer knew the other guys in the car weren't local. The cop asked the carnie where he got the weed. Without hesitation, he turned around and pointed at me. So I got hauled to the police station. They roughed me up a bit and tried to scare me, threatening to send me to prison for the rest of my life. I had attitude and told them something to the effect of, "Yeah, right. I don't think so. I'm only 14." They ended up calling my mom and released me without pressing charges. My mom was not happy, but I didn't get in much trouble that time.

The carnie who ratted me out also told the cops where my brother's friend lived. So they arrested my brother's friend, too, who assumed that I was the one who squealed. I was many things, but I was not a snitch. I never saw the carnies again.

The small town cops-know-everyone vibe of Ferndale in the '70s did not work to my advantage. The cops knew who was in the partying crowd and kept tabs on us.

That was far from the only time I was busted for marijuana possession. About six months after the carnie incident, a few buddies and I were partying in a room at a local motel with beer and two or three bags of marijuana. Suddenly, someone pounded loudly on the door, soon followed by a loud thud as the door was kicked in, and half a dozen cops rushed toward us. The way they came at us, it felt like they thought we were a bunch of drug kingpins. Far from that, we were just a bunch of irresponsible, stoned high school kids. They acted like it was a big drug bust, even though, at the most, they got a few ounces of marijuana. We didn't have any hardcore drugs, so it was a lot of drama for a relatively minor infraction. This isn't to say that marijuana isn't a serious drug – it is!

My run-ins with the law didn't always involve drugs and alcohol. My next interaction with law enforcement happened when our neighbor called the cops on me for riding my dirt bike around the cul-de-sac where we lived. I still didn't have a driver's license, and the bike was not street-legal, so I was breaking the law. Compared to my other illegal activities, this was nothing.

I went to extreme lengths to get drugs. In Chapter One I mentioned breaking into houses. I would also use my disability to get doctors to write me prescriptions for drugs. I had also gotten into self-harm to try to get pain medication, usually Vicodin. Once I ran over my foot with my truck.

Another time I dropped a 20-pound weight on my foot so it would bruise and swell. An addict will go to any length to get their fix. I remember driving 150 miles each way just to pick up some drugs to get high one time.

The police would soon hit us with a vengeance. It turned out our little gang wasn't so tough after all. Several of my friends were caught and arrested for the thefts. They snitched on the rest of us, thinking it would reduce their sentences. The police hauled us all in, and each of us faced five or six counts of burglary.

A couple of us were just shy of 18 and were tried as adults; others were underage and went to juvenile detention and then to prison for minors.

With the assistance of a court-appointed attorney, I plea-bargained the six counts of burglary down to one. I received a 90-day sentence in an adult facility. It would be the first of many times I would be in jail with adults.

When I started my sentence, I found out that I could become a trustee, which amounts to being a jail employee. I worked in the janitorial and food service departments of the jail. Perks for trustees included the possibility of a reduced sentence and other benefits such as extra food at mealtime. Being a trustee and on good behavior reduced my stay to "only" 45 days.

I hated being in jail, but all told, I got by reasonably well. I never had problems with other inmates, and I learned that good humor and laughter would make the days pass faster. When I was released, I was convinced I would never go back to jail, but that is not how things would unfold. Once you get caught up in the destructive cycle of addiction, crime, arrest, and jail time, it becomes tough to break. For many, the pattern results in death, and I only have Jesus to thank that it didn't go that far for me.

My careless and destructive behavior resumed right after I left jail. Of the many stupid things I've done that could have killed me, one happened then when my friends and I ventured into Puget Sound - now called the Salish Sea - to visit the San Juan Islands. We loaded into a 12-foot wooden rowboat built in 1959 that had never once been in the water.

We only packed the things we thought we'd need – tents, clothes, food, weed, cocaine, and 151-proof alcohol. Keep in mind this was the first time in my life I had ever set foot in a boat and that I was not a strong swimmer. If there was ever a recipe for disaster, we had it. I felt uneasy about the trip but ignored those feelings and went along anyway.

We strapped a 7.5 horsepower engine on the back and, at 6:30 PM, set off into the yonder. We launched from Sandy Point, a peninsula near Ferndale that juts out and south from the mainland.

My friends started drinking heavily right away, to the point where two of them passed out about 45 minutes after we started. This meant that I had to steer the boat with zero navigation experience, no map, and in waters I had only seen from a distance.

I did not drink alcohol on the whole trip; instead, I plied myself with cocaine and marijuana. The boat had a small hole and began taking on water immediately. Fortunately, there was a bucket on board, so we continued anyway and bailed the water as it filled the bottom of the boat.

What should have been a three to four-hour trip took us almost eight hours, meaning we were out in the middle of the Georgia Strait in the middle of the night with only the starlight and a small crescent moon illuminating the water. It was probably the most scared I had ever been at any point in my life, which is saying a lot considering all the foolish and dangerous things I had done. I prayed nonstop the entire crossing.

When I looked up into a sky with no light pollution, the stars were spectacular. In the water below, the phosphorus shimmered an electric blue. Even in that dark hour, God's creation was on glorious display. It was truly breathtaking.

After passing almost the entire night slowly zig-zagging through the sea, we arrived at Matia Island. To this day, I have no idea how we made it there at all, and I only have God to thank that we did. Matia is a 145-acre island in the northwest portion of the San Juan Archipelago. The entire island and the water immediately surrounding it is a protected state park.

When I jumped off the boat to tie it up, I slipped on a wet log and fell hard to the ground, landing on my left wrist. I heard it snap. I knew that moment that I had broken my wrist. I was in an incredible amount of pain.

Despite the agony of my injury, all I wanted to do was sleep. Somehow I managed to pitch my tent only using my right arm, climbed in, and quickly fell asleep.

We slept only a few hours as the bright morning light came quickly. We spent that next day exploring nearby Sucia Island, another island that is 100% state park. It was a truly beautiful place to see another aspect of God's creation mostly untouched by human development.

After a day of exploring, we made it back to the boat only to discover that almost all of our food had been stolen. It was time to head home. Almost immediately after we set off in our rickety boat, the wind began to blow hard, and a soft rain turned into a downpour. The sea erupted in six to eight-foot swells, which nearly capsized the tiny boat on several occasions. Again, I prayed fervently. Had the boat flipped, all of us would have surely drowned.

Between the rain and the small hole in the boat, we took on quite a bit of water. I bailed, prayed, bailed, prayed, repeat. In those moments, death seemed inevitable. Somehow we made it back to Sandy Point. Once again, God saved me.

After the number of things that could have gone even worse on our "cruise", I'm fortunate to be alive. The entire trip was nothing but mayhem and chaos.

I have a lot of history in Sandy Point. Not only was it the launching point for our ill-advised adventure, but it's also where I currently live. Tragically, shortly after our boat trip, one of my friends committed suicide at Sandy Point by pointing a shotgun at his head and pulling the trigger. I have many memories here now – some good, some awful. Life is worth living. If you or someone you know has severe depression, please seek help – call a crisis line, the pastor of your church, or even me. There is a world of support out there, and you are truly loved.

The broken wrist I got on the boat trip was severe enough to require surgery. My bone had shattered in several places. The doctors removed and replaced them with a silastic implant. Unfortunately, my body rejected the implant and I ended up having my wrist fused.

To this day, it's a huge mess. At some point in the future, I may need to have reconstructive surgery. In addition to the ongoing pain from the injury, my wrist has also become arthritic. It was the price I paid for not listening to my gut when it told me to stay behind on the boat trip. But I am thankful I survived at all, and who knows what would have happened to my friends had I not gone along. The good Lord always has a plan.

Like a magnet for drama and bad fortune, not long after the boat trip, I got into a fight with a so-called friend who owed me $800. I was high on Vicodin from a prescription I obtained after the surgery for my broken wrist. I was carrying a .38 revolver at the time because I was regularly running marijuana shipments between Whatcom County and Eastern Washington. When I ran into this "friend", I said, "Where's my money?" He said he wouldn't pay me, so I pulled out my gun and stuck it in his face.

"Okay! Okay! I'll pay you!" he yelled.

Being amped-up on the Vicoden, I screamed at him, "You're lucky I don't shoot you right now and leave you lying in the street!" Then I walked away. I would never have shot him, but I did want to scare him enough so he would pay me. Of course, when there is a firearm involved, things can easily go awry. God protected both of us that day.

He called the police to report the incident. They arrested me and charged me with assault with a deadly weapon, a crime that carried a 10-year maximum sentence. I got off with a plea deal by pleading guilty to felony possession of a firearm. I received a six-month sentence.

And thus, the vicious cycle continued. All told, my constant run-ins with the law would eventually have me spending a total of around three and a half years of my life in prison and on probation for over ten.

The punishments for my actions were sometimes more subtle than jail or probation. There were constant fines and then repercussions for not paying those fines. One such repercussion is putting your driver's license on hold when you don't pay your fines. Of course, that never kept me from driving.

During this time in my life, I was emotionally unstable and prone to violence. My drug-using friends and I would often go to the town of Birch Bay on the Canadian border just to pick fights with Canadians. We didn't care that we were destroying property, hurting people, and wreaking havoc. I remember bashing people in the face with beer bottles and using baseball bats to smash into their bodies. I give thanks that I never paralyzed or killed anyone, although I do know I was the cause of many broken bones and hospital visits. Once I broke a man's arm in three different places. I'm glad I'm not that person today.

Corinthians 5:17: "Therefore, if anyone is in Christ, the new creation has come: The old has gone, the new is here!"

The toll of addictions and poor choices can be heartwrenching. They affect health, friendships, finances, employment, general enjoyment of life, and destroy families.

My parents have both been gone for many years, and to this day, I miss them dearly. They often wanted to do cool, fun things with me, but I constantly declined because I only wanted to do drugs. I deeply regret that. I would give anything to spend time with them now. When I had the chance, I chose my addictions instead.

I was 27 when my father passed away. The only time in my life my father ever told me he was proud of me was when my son, Loren Jr., was born. My dad said he was thankful that I named my son Loren Jr. because it was his dad's name. My fondest memory of my father is when he accepted Jesus as his savior. That happened a short two weeks before his death. I do find some comfort knowing I will see my dad again in heaven. His absence in my life certainly left a void. I wish I had gotten to know him better.

The demons of addiction rip through one's life with the destructive force of a tornado. But God is always there watching over us with an invitation for recovery and a righteous life.

God was not the only one watching over me. At one point, it turned out that narcotics officers had me under surveillance.

We had been doing drugs in a motel the night before. The police had been monitoring for drug activity. I was a small fish as far as the drug trade goes, but to catch the big fish, they watch the low-level users like me on the street.

You can only escape the consequences of your decisions for so long. Some people on the street felt that the judicial system would go easier on them if they ratted other people out. In the end, we all have to pay for our actions, though. There is never an easy way out. If you do the crime, you need to do the time. Bad choices have inescapable, harmful consequences, and facing them straight on is the only way to learn from your mistakes.

To understand and recover, it's essential to recognize that we live in a fallen world. It's a story that began in the Garden of Eden and continues through to this day. Had Adam and Eve not chosen sin, human history would have been entirely different.

Yes, the pain is real. We've all experienced it. But it's still okay because of the love that Jesus holds for all of us.

Matthew 7:7: "Ask, and it will be given to you. Search, and you will find. Knock, and the door will be opened to you."

John 3:16: "God so loved the world that he gave his one and only Son. Anyone who believes in him will not die but will have eternal life."

Psalm 37:4: "Find your delight in the Lord. Then he will give you everything your heart really wants."

Psalm 56:3: "When I'm afraid, I put my trust in you."

If you are in pain, it is okay to cry out to Jesus. Ask Him to come into your heart. He will meet you right where you are and save you. I besiege you to give your life to Christ before another day goes by. You will never regret that decision. It won't remove all the pain and challenges in your life, but you will not confront them alone.

On the contrary, you will go forth alongside the most powerful force in the universe: the love of God. In spite of all I have gone through, my faith is still strong. I trust Him. I thank Him every day for the life I am blessed to live. Hurt people don't have to hurt other people. We have a choice. We can be menders.

I have learned to take my troubles as they come. I can now maintain my composure amid distraction and temptation. I have learned that if I can rise above my circumstances amid the distressing things of life, I'll be okay by His grace. I believe those are gifts from God.

There once was an Olympic diving athlete who always put his foot in the water before climbing the diving platform. When asked about this habit, he told a story of going alone to practice after hours at a local pool. Only the security lights were on, but the moon shone brightly through the windows. He climbed up to the top platform and walked out on the diving board, raising his arms high in the air, then at 90-degree angles at his sides. When he did this, he glanced down, and the moon cast a shadow of the Cross to the bottom of the pool. The water had been drained from the pool, and he didn't realize it until that moment. Had he dived, the impact would have killed him instantly. He knew that the cross that saved his life and was a sign, and from that moment forth, he gave his life to Jesus Christ. Every time after that, when he would go diving, he would dip his foot into the pool to assure himself there was water in it. There is power in the blood of Jesus Christ.

Hebrews 13:5: "I will never leave you. I will never desert you."

He has always been by me, has never left me, and has never forsaken me. He has held me in the palm of his hands since the day I was born.

Chapter 4

Blessings and Tribulations

"We live by believing, not by seeing."
Corinthians 5:7

As I write these words, my partner, Teresa, and I are sneaking up on our seventh anniversary, all truly by the Grace of God. We have two beautiful children. She is my best friend and the love of my life. I have never met such a wonderful woman. I think she knows me better than I know myself.

Before Teresa, I dated and had been with many other women but did not have the tools or maturity to have a healthy romantic relationship.

In high school, I went out with a girl named Kelly. She was a cute, bubbly, blonde cheerleader. We dated for a while; we were classmates until she broke up with me. It was my first big heartbreak.

My first wife's name was Sharon. We met in 1976 and married in 1978. Our relationship involved years of heartache, cheating, and lies. But some blessings did come out of our marriage – our two beautiful children.

Not long after Sharon and I married, I knew I had made a colossal mistake. I was also making massive mistakes on other fronts.

It was around that time that I got caught forging prescriptions for narcotics. When my case went to trial, the judge sentenced me to six months in prison. Even without the other issues in our marriage, that would have been an enormous obstacle.

About a year and a half into our marriage, Sharon left me for her sister's husband's brother. I didn't even realize she had been unfaithful until I drove down the road one day and spotted half our possessions stuffed into the man's station wagon. I never saw it coming.

Like a redneck stereotype out of Hollywood, I picked up my baseball bat, jumped into my four-wheel-drive Chevy pickup truck, and headed out to take care of business. He lived in a cabin up a long meandering road in the wilderness surrounding Mt. Baker. I think that was the angriest I have ever been in my life.

When I arrived at the cabin, I gathered all my rage and strength and, in one burst, kicked in the front door of the place. Even I was shocked I was able to do that!

We started shouting back and forth, me holding the baseball bat in the air and promising to rain fury on their deception, dishonesty, and betrayal. They insisted nothing had happened. I yelled at the top of my lungs that they were disgusting liars. In my wrath, using every ounce of strength I could muster, I bashed the guy with my bat. Had he not covered his head with his arms, he would probably be dead.

"I could have killed him!" I shouted at Sharon. "You're lucky I don't hit you with this thing, too!" I yelled.

Looking back at how I saw things in those days, I thought that Sharon, being my wife, made her my property. I am not proud of the way I reacted. It was not a situation where violence and unrestrained anger could have helped in any way. Since those days, I have learned how to deal more constructively with strong emotions. Now I can resolve potentially explosive situations with patience, prayer, and using my brain instead of my brawn.

Nobody reported the incident in the cabin, so I never faced arrest or charges for the break-in, threats of violence, or assault. I probably deserved to be arrested, though.

The dust needed to settle, so it took several years for Sharon and me to be in contact again. When we did reconnect, we tried to restore our relationship. Our emotions ran strong - there was so much hurt, betrayal, anger, and lust. We definitely did not have a Christ-centered relationship. We gave it another try. At one point, Sharon announced she was pregnant and wanted me to pay for an abortion. I firmly refused.

I have always considered abortion a moral evil. However, I am not free of sin in this regard. In high school, I got a girl pregnant and agreed to an abortion. For this, I have asked God repeatedly for forgiveness. I know that I have been forgiven. Nonetheless, I consider that abortion one of the greatest mistakes I have ever made, which is saying a lot. I have made so many mistakes!

Our first child was born in 1983. She was a girl, and we named her Tangela. I always liked the name Angela, but it was such a common name in those days. I wanted something that stood out a bit more, so I put a "T" in front of it.

The following year we had our second child, Loren Jr.

By the time we finally got back together, I had found a level of forgiveness for Sharon. This went a long way in making it possible to patch and mend parts of our marriage, but it wasn't enough. After moving in together again, a bitterness rose from within me. I had more forgiving to do, and I needed to own my responsibility for our issues. I did neither of these, so our relationship continued down its rocky, conflict-laden path.

However, even as Sharon and I tried to make things work, my heart had moved on. I was in love with my sister-in-law's daughter, Jeannie. Jeannie and I never did get together, and she was dating a friend of mine. But this complicated things in my head and heart.

Between my insecurity, immaturity, constant state of intoxication, and inability to create a stable, healthy relationship, my life's painful, vicious up-and-down patterns continued. One of the main reasons Sharon and I got back together and tried to work things out was for the children's sake. In hindsight, this was a big mistake.

Years later, when I was in prison, Sharon cheated on me again with the same man.

Despite our long history of dysfunction and drama, Sharon holds a special place in my heart. She is, after all, the mother of two of my children. But in my day-to-day life, she is the mother of my children and nothing more.

It felt like a black cloud followed me around. I went from one crisis to the next, feeling like a victim and blaming everyone but myself for my problems. "The system did that to me!" I would tell myself. Or, "My probation officer was the problem!" Whenever I got caught, I thought it was someone else's fault. I was not what you would call a productive member of society.

Despite my utter lack of self-worth, I kept my faith in Jesus and belief in a good and just God. It was just buried under my fears, addictions, dramas, and destructive life patterns.

Even as I blamed everyone but me for my problems, I simultaneously knew that I had to take responsibility at some point. If for nothing else, I needed to do this for my children. The mind can work in funny and contradictory ways. In a moment of some clarity, I swore off alcohol and stopped drinking for many years. Unfortunately, I did not apply that clarity to narcotics, which I continued to consume.

Shortly after my Tangela's birth, Sharon had a severe accident sledding on Mount Baker while riding an inner tube. She broke several vertebrae after falling into a tree well. The ski patrol was called-in to perform the rescue. As I waited there in the snow for hour after agonizing hour for them to arrive, dig her out, treat her, and wait for an ambulance to come, I looked at Sharon with compassion for the first time since we had met.

She spent over a week in the hospital, leaving me alone in our house to take care of our 3-month-old baby girl. In this way, the sledding accident had a silver lining. During this time with Tangela, we formed a deep bond. This would set a precedent for my relationship when Loren Jr. came along, too.

I knew the moment my son was born that his name would be Loren Jr. Like me, I wanted him to be named after his grandparents.

It took Sharon several months to heal from the accident. Things went quite well between us during her recovery – probably the most "normal" it had ever been.

Tangela and Loren Jr. were the most positive experiences I had up to this point in my life. However, this does not negate the fact that having children when you have the emotional maturity of a 14-year-old is a recipe for disaster. Tangela and Loren Jr. grew up in a toxic environment. The fallout from my addictions affected my children in a myriad of ways. In addition to witnessing my destructive behaviors, I did not provide the level of care I would have given if I had been sober. My lifestyle affected everything from our finances to our diet. And my various stints in prison didn't help either.

I feel a tremendous amount of remorse for making such poor choices. Despite the dysfunction that surrounded them, both children also knew they were loved. And as a credit to them, they also developed their own sets of positive morals and values. At one point, Sharon and her family accused me of physically abusing the children. I was shocked by the accusation as it could not have been more untrue. I disproved it in part through a lie detector test, but the ordeal left a sour taste in my mouth toward my in-laws.

There were some bright spots. Tangela and Loren became involved in sports, and I helped out as a volunteer and a coach. At one point or another, they played baseball, basketball, and soccer. One year I coached all three sports and was fortunate to have both my children on teams I coached. Another bright spot was our family trip in 1989 to Bakersfield, California, to visit my sister, followed by a full day in Disneyland. I'd rank our day at Disneyland as one of the best and most fun days of my entire life.

Because of my poor choices, I had built the rest of my life on toxicity, guilt, shame, hurt, disgust, pain, and misery. I did not realize that God was building a life worth living. I think the biggest sin one can commit is not putting Jesus first.

Along with addiction, I also struggled with health problems; some related to CMT, some not. Throughout my life, I've had around two dozen surgeries. I often used the prescribed painkillers to feed my addictions rather than to heal and treat the pain. Sometimes I would sell the medications to pay for other drugs.

Once I got a severe staph infection. I had feared needles up to that point in my life, but my treatment involved an IV line that basically went straight into my heart. It was attached to a bag of antibiotic fluid housed in a fanny pack. I had to carry that contraption around for about six months, and by the end of the treatment my fear of needles had evaporated. When I was introduced to heroin down the road, the fact that I had overcome my fear of needles became a curse.

My addiction got utterly out of control in the mid-1980s while my kids were still young. My first stint in federal prison was not a direct result of drugs, theft, or violence. It was because of an honest mistake on my part.

I was working at a local food processing plant. At work one day, I fell down a flight of slick stairs and crushed two discs in my lower back. I already suffered from scoliosis, so the fall compounded my pain and suffering. I received worker's compensation for the injury. At the time, I was also receiving a small social security benefit for my CMT disability, which made me ineligible for the worker's compensation benefit. I didn't realize that by accepting both, I was committing a crime.

The federal government would later charge me with fraud. They wanted to make an example out of me, and I was sentenced to two years in federal prison. When the sentence was passed down, U.S. Marshals carrying M16s literally ripped my four-year-old daughter out of my arms and took me into custody. They weren't messing around.

You would have thought I was a dangerous criminal or a presidential assassin by how they handled me. A profound sense of dread, abandonment, pain, and fear washed over me. Fear tends to perpetuate more fear, and so it did within me – escalating to a point I had never experienced before.

My anxiety levels went through the roof, and I felt utterly hopeless. I thought there was a good chance my life would end in a prison cell and that I would likely never see my family again. I lost a little piece of my heart on that day. My numerous sins seemed to have caught up with me.

I would spend the next 17 months, 11 days, and 7 hours in the federal prison system.

The first prison was In Tacoma. I spent two weeks there. Then they put me on a plane bound for a federal penitentiary in Portland, Oregon. For a young man from a small town who had never flown before, to take that first airplane journey in handcuffs and shackles was certainly not the way I imagined it would be. I was so scared! I prayed the entire flight. I was seated next to a drug smuggler from Puerto Rico.

The plane was part of a fleet of confiscated aircraft seized in drug busts. And it would be one of many such flights. If you have ever seen the movie Con Air, they get a lot of it right about what it's like on the airplanes that fly convicts.

On one flight on a 727, I sat next to a guy from Tacoma who worked for Boeing on the 727 assembly line. He said he and his coworkers would get drunk between shifts. Sometimes, they would go out on the wing and sleep or pass out. Considering I was already afraid of flying, his stories did not inspire confidence in the endeavor.

In the federal prison system, they usually place you in a facility far away from your family. It's just one of the ways they psychologically abuse inmates under their authority.

After Portland, they flew me to a facility in Boise, Idaho. The jail there was so old they still had pictures of Jesse James on the wall. It was 1987, but it felt like I had been transported back to the 1800s. It was surreal! The facility was disgusting and decrepit, so I was grateful when they transferred me to a prison in Salt Lake City.

They only kept me in Salt Lake for a short time before my next flight on "Con Air" to El Reno, Oklahoma. The facility in El Reno was a level-five maximum security prison.

You must be selective about who you trust in the prison system. It is full of criminals, after all. They will take anything from you. Typically, the authorities take your shoes when you get to prison, but they let me keep mine because my disability affected my feet. A couple of guys hustled me out of my shoes before I even got to El Reno.

When I arrived at El Reno, the temperature was hovering around -10 degrees Fahrenheit, and there were a couple of feet of snow on the ground. The prison cells were long, dark gray, and stacked five levels high.

The system treated me like a hardened adult criminal, but inside was an emotionally stunted, immature, insecure little boy with a disability. When I heard the jail cell clang shut that first night In El Reno, I thought my life was over and that I would never see my family or friends ever again. I had heard cell doors close before in county jails, but this one echoed through every ounce of my being.

I was utterly devastated and felt an immense depression come over me. I spent two long, cold months in El Reno.

My next destination was Terminal Island, California, off the coast of Long Beach. It's a mostly artificial island that is home to a federal correctional institution, a United States Coast Guard base, private shipyards, and a few seafood canneries. When I was there in 1986, it was also home to the Long Beach Naval Shipyard, which used to occupy half the island and has since been decommissioned.

The Queen Mary is docked just a few miles away on an adjacent artificial peninsula. From the prison, you could see the fireworks they would set off every night all summer long by the former trans-Atlantic ocean liner that now served as a luxury hotel.

I met a celebrity at Terminal Island. John Delorian, the man who invented the futuristic stainless steel car made famous in the movie Back to the Future; he was serving time there for cocaine possession. I was introduced to him in the prison yard when a fellow inmate pointed him out to me. Delorian was just standing there calmly smoking a cigarette.

It was a little bit of a relief to be on the West Coast. I was geographically closer to my family, and it was a reasonable distance for them to travel to visit me. My brother Marvin and his wife's daughter, Jeannie, came to visit me there. They wouldn't let Jeannie into the prison because she was dressed in a halter-top, which was against policy because showing so much skin could overstimulate the prisoners and cause a disturbance. As I mentioned earlier, I had a crush on Jeannie, so seeing her while in prison would have been a treat. It bummed me out. But I did get to visit my brother, which offered a bit of fresh air to my stagnant existence behind the prison's walls.

When you are in the federal prison system, you have to work. I ended up in the paint shop making $0.12 an hour. Despite the poor pay, the work kept me busy and made the time go by faster.

My cellmate was a convicted murderer serving a lifetime sentence. I slept with one eye open. Needless to say, I was grateful when I was transferred from Terminal Island. My next stint was at a prison camp near Boron, California. It was near Edward's Air Force Base in the middle of the Mojave Desert. This relatively small, minimum-security prison had no walls or guard towers surrounding it, but there was an FAA radar facility towering above the facility. Boron housed around 500 inmates, and life there was a little more tolerable than the other federal prisons I stayed in.

Jets from the Air Force base would fly so low you could feel the heat from the engines. I watched stealth bombers doing training exercises before the public even knew about them.

Even the food was decent at Boron. For the most part, we could eat as much as we wanted from the pasta bar, potato bar, and salad bar. Inmates often called these more relaxed prisons Club Fed. It's where white collar criminals did their time. Ivan Boesky, the multi-millionaire caught in an insider stock trading scandal in the mid-1980s, served his sentence at Boron.

The accommodations at Boron were 4-person rooms, but I usually only had one roommate in mine. It filled to capacity only once or twice while I was there. We had a swimming pool, which was great because it was so hot in the desert. I was also baptized in that pool! We snuck out of our bunkhouse in the early morning twilight to perform the ritual. There were a lot of believers in Boron. We had church up on a hill with a full-time pastor. I mostly hung out with fellow believers.

The prison fellowship was started by Chuck Colson, former President Richard Nixon's attorney. Colson served as Special Counsel to Nixon and went to prison for obstruction of justice in the aftermath of the Watergate scandal. Colson found what he called his "religious awakening" while he was in jail.

Another perk of minimum-security federal prisons is that they allow furloughs. Me and six other guys all got to go. We stayed in private homes with host families. The family I stayed with was very friendly and lived near Disneyland. They were not able to take me inside the theme park, but we went close by. This was before I had taken my kids to Disneyland. They also took us to a Los Angeles Dodgers baseball game.

Following the game, they had the biggest and most

exhilarating fireworks show I had ever seen. We got to lie on the green of the baseball field on blankets as we watched the explosive display. It was a beautiful California evening.

That same evening I swore off using drugs for the rest of my life. Although my intent was pure, my understanding of addiction was incomplete. I did not yet have the tools to keep that promise to myself and stay clean. I think I knew even as I made that decision that my chances of success were remote. But in my heart, I knew what I wanted.

The prison fellowship helps needy families rebuild their homes. My group helped reconstruct a woman's house that had been rented out and trashed by the renters. The effort was organized by a host church, the Evangelical Free Church of Southern California. The pastor there was one of my mentors, Charles (Chuck) Swindoll. I had the opportunity to give my testimony in front of the congregation, which numbered over 7,500 people. I had difficulty talking in front of five people, so this was quite a leap for me. The experience was a blessing. I had the honor to meet Chuck Swindoll, a man I have looked up to for most of my Christian life. He is a great man of God. I have read many of his books and listened to his sermons on "Insights for Living".

It is remarkable what God can do when people pull together. We rebuilt the woman's house from top to bottom.

It was also nice to have a break from prison, and I felt grateful to be chosen for the furlough program. My job at Boron was running the laundry. The inmates wore khakis and shirts that were hand-me-downs from the military. Once a week, inmates could exchange their clothing, and we would wash it and put it back in rotation. It was a good job as far as federal prisons go.

43

The federal government closed the Boron Federal Prison in 2000 due to budget cuts.

I know now that God was always holding my hand, even during my darkest days in federal prison. I don't understand God, but I do love him. Evelyn Underhill, a prolific author on spiritual topics, wrote, "If God were small enough to be understood, He would not be big enough to be worshipped." I could not agree more.

As much as prison represented a huge loss for me, my addictions probably would have killed me if I had not been there. Furthermore, I never would have met my mentor, Chuck Swindoll, let alone give my testimony to over 7,000 people.

Despite my shortcomings, my priority was to walk with Christ. Although Christ was working in my life, I would soon turn my back on Him again.

Chapter 5

Narcotics and Angels

**"I'm worn out from calling for help.
My throat is very dry.
My eyes grow tired looking for my God."
Psalm 63:3**

When I got out of federal prison, the many commitments I made to myself to go on the straight and narrow went by the wayside. Once out, I reconnected with my old friends, and two weeks later, I was using again. I felt like a complete failure.

The disease of addiction is cunning, baffling, and powerful. It would take many more years for me to be redeemed by complete and total surrender. Being a stubborn person, asking for help was never an option.

God has carried me through my trials and tribulations, but He never plucked me out of them. He always gave me the grace to carry through. In my heart, I knew my life would turn out okay. It took me many more years of suffering to get to where He wanted my life to be. If one cannot make good choices in life, choices will be made for you. For sure, this was the case in my life.

Hebrews 4:15: "We have a high priest who can feel it when we are weak and hurting."

Guilt says, "I did something wrong." Shame says, "I am something wrong." I could not get enough of what I craved, be it sex, money, drugs, or food. I never felt satisfied, and my addictions always asked for more.

Many times throughout my years of addiction, I talked about getting clean. I made promises to my wife, my parents, my children, and myself. I simply did not have the willpower. And what little resolve I had diminished over the years of degrading my body and mind.

God wants to get our attention, and He will do all that He can to get it. For sure, God has always tried to get my attention.

Hebrews 12:6: "Because the Lord disciplines the one he loves, and he chastens everyone he accepts as his son."

Revelation 3:12: "The one who is victorious I will make a pillar in the temple of my God. Never again will they leave it. I will write on them the name of my God and the name of the city of my God, the new Jerusalem, which is coming down out of heaven from my God; and I will also write on them my new name."

Revelation 3:19: "Those whom I love I rebuke and discipline. So be earnest and repent."

My doctor at the time was a pain specialist in Seattle. To address the severe pain associated with my CMT, he admitted me to the hospital for a week, where they prescribed fentanyl and oxycodone. Both of these drugs are opioids and potent narcotics, although fentanyl is far stronger than oxycodone. Neither drug had been fully approved by the FDA yet, so my treatment was part of a study to see how they worked and what protocols worked best. I was, in essence, a guinea pig for their dangerous and high-stakes lab experiment. They even paid me $350 for my participation, which was a lot of money for a homeless person!

They gave me all the fentanyl and oxycontin I could use, which essentially meant that I was sedated and loaded on narcotics for the whole week. The hospital provided as much food as I could eat at any time of the day or night. I pigged out on pizza, hot dogs, and hamburgers, sometimes ordering at 3 a.m.

The study continued after my hospital stay, meaning I was still a guinea pig in their experiment. To get the drugs, I had to travel to Seattle each month to pick up my supply. I don't recall exactly how many pills they gave me every month, but I think it was around 100. Providing free, highly addictive drugs to a drug addict probably wasn't the best idea.

Once I took the Greyhound from Bellingham to Seattle to fill my prescription. I ran to catch the return bus, and the next thing I remember was being awakened by the bus driver. We were at the bus station in Everett, about a third of the way back to Bellingham. I was sprawled out across the back seats, with pills spilled all over the seats and floor.

My downward spiral continued over the next 24 hours. I met up with a friend in Bellingham, and we got hold of some cocaine. We spent the night snorting cocaine and taking oxycontin.

As I stumbled around downtown Bellingham, I ran into two girls I knew. I was completely out of it. They took me to a gas station where one of them ran to a pay phone and called 911. (This was long before everyone had cell phones.) The paramedics soon showed up and, given my condition, said they needed to take me to the hospital. I steadfastly refused their request and told them to leave me alone. One paramedic insisted he take my blood pressure, and I relented. He took it, and it was 190 over 0 – I was literally in the process of dying. They rushed me to the hospital.

Not surprisingly, I had overdosed on the combination of cocaine and oxycontin. I spent over a week in the hospital recovering, in part because I had developed pneumonia.

The Angels had watched over me again. Had I not run into the girls, had they not called 911, and had I refused the paramedic's offer to take my blood pressure, I would have died that night.

I have had pneumonia five times over my lifetime, each with its corresponding trip to and recovery in the hospital. There are so many times I had been close to death, and each time God had something greater in store for my life, so He didn't take me.

Opioid addiction would go on to kill over half a million people in the United States. Fentanyl, oxycodone, and later Oxycontin were the main drivers of the pandemic. Oxycontin was a 12-hour release version of oxycodone released in 1995 and was marketed by Purdue Pharma as a "safer" pain medication. As I write this chapter, Purdue Pharma has been dissolved in a bankruptcy settlement stemming from their irresponsible and deadly criminal behavior in marketing these highly addictive and dangerous painkillers. I thank the Lord I was not another death statistic in that saga. I know beyond a shadow of a doubt that I'm alive today because God watches over me and has sent His Angels to protect me. I am forever grateful for His love.

Lying in that hospital bed, I once again swore off drugs and alcohol. It was yet one more vain attempt to do something I did not yet have the strength, tools, or faith to pull off. I know there are people who have been delivered from the depths of darkness and addiction by fully surrendering their lives to God. My brother had been able to pull off such a recovery, but I was not someone who could do that. I simply was not capable. I needed a helping hand, a program, the tools, and to be taught how to use those tools.

Shortly after my release from the hospital, a longtime friend who was a wealthy developer rented me an apartment in one of his new complexes in Bellingham. I was able to get Section 8 federal housing assistance to pay for it. I ended up with a three-bedroom unit all to myself, which was a drastic change from being homeless and on the street, let alone my time in crowded jails and prisons.

I felt grateful to have a place to call home. Returning to a safe, warm place every night was a luxury I had missed. Sadly, it wasn't enough of an impetus to give up my destructive lifestyle.

Over the years, I did make many feeble attempts at trying recovery programs. I would enter them with the intention of getting clean, but then I would meet other addicts there. When I had the urge to get another fix, they knew where to score more drugs, and the vicious cycle would begin anew. I usually lasted about three days sober, but on day four, the withdrawal symptoms are so powerful that you wish you were dead. Getting loaded again was the easy way to avoid feeling that level of pain and despair.

During this part of my life, I switched addictions from alcohol to pain medication. At the time, doctors prescribed Percocet and Vicodin as if they were candy. I hatched a crazy plan to write my own prescriptions, which I was caught doing. I was now looking at my third felony. I received another six months in jail.

I would have gotten off with a slap on the hand had I become an informant. I believed even then that if you did the crime and got caught, you should do the time. Also, I just wasn't about to rat out other addicts, something that would not have gone down well in the streets anyway. I would not have thought twice about informing on someone who raped a woman, hurt a child, or committed another violent act towards an innocent person.

One would think I had learned my lesson, but I was arrested yet again for prescription forgery. My punishment was yet another six months in the slammer.

I fully intended to stay clean and sober upon my release. I managed for about six months, but I did not yet have the strength to succeed. I was immature and had few life skills. This was a pattern for me – get caught, go to jail, commit to changing my ways, and then revert to my old habits.

There would be many more short and long-term prison stays before I was finally able to stay sober and leave my destructive lifestyle behind.

Of my many attempts at sobriety, the longest during that period of my life lasted from 1992 to 1998. This was after I divorced Sharon. Our children were teenagers at the time. Over those six years, I started and built a cleaning business. I had a good life then. It was a life worth living.

I was soon due for another surgery on my foot, which would again mean more pain medication and another chance for me to throw myself into the throes of addiction. I deluded myself into believing that this time would be different and that I would take only enough drugs to address the immediate physical pain from the surgery. The surgery went well at first, but then the pain grew so severe that I justified taking two to three pain meds every four hours, far exceeding the dosage the doctor prescribed. The doctors cut me off, but a friend gave me a bag of heroin and told me there was more where that had come from.

That same friend died a couple of years ago. He was able to kick heroin by going through a Suboxone protocol to reduce the withdrawal symptoms. But he kept drinking heavily and died of a heart attack. He should have lived a longer life, but his addictions destroyed his body. It's beyond sad.

Heroin can be injected with a needle into a vein or muscle or even directly under the skin. On the street, injecting directly into a vein is called mainlining. If you inject under the skin, it's called skin-popping.

Heroin is a lot cheaper than oxycontin, too. I could buy a bag of heroin for $20, where oxycontin could cost thousands of dollars on the street.

Soon, my 3-bedroom apartment became a drug house filled with crackheads and heroin addicts. At any time of the day or night, addicts were coming, going, getting wasted, passed out on the floor, arguing, talking, laughing, or dealing.

Despite my partying lifestyle, I did my best to make an honest living. I poured myself into a workaholic life running the janitorial business. For a whole four-year period, I took no vacations. I worked seven nights a week to keep it afloat, sometimes working all night long. To stay awake and maintain my energy levels, I would snort cocaine.

A buddy and I once spent about 10 days doing cocaine. We didn't sleep the whole duration. After a time, I experienced what is called cocaine psychosis where the brain loses the ability to think clearly, discern reality, or function properly. It's absolutely brutal. A buddy of mine suggested we get some heroin to come down off the cocaine. He injected first, and then I did some a few minutes later. Suddenly, I looked at my friend and saw him appear to shape-shift into what looked like a demon. It was probably the most intense thing I've ever seen. His whole body swelled up like a balloon. People panicked. This was very real! His heart appeared to give out, and he tumbled over onto the floor. I recognized what was happening and immediately performed CPR. Someone freaked out and called 911. The cops showed up quickly and grabbed me. "You need to tell us right now what your friend is on because if he dies, you're going downtown with us."

I told them about the heroin, and they were able to save him. It was one of the scariest moments of my life.

I spent most of my life running from God, not toward Him. He has kept me alive for His glory even in the worst of times.

When I lived in the three-bedroom apartment, I subleased rooms to other junkies but most never paid rent because they spent all their money on drugs. Sometimes they would give me drugs instead, but you can't pay rent with heroin or cocaine. Since I couldn't pay the bills, utility shutoff notices were the norm.

One time my girlfriend stole a relatively large amount of heroin and cocaine from a guy we knew. As we were using that night, a brake drum from my car came crashing through our bedroom window. I thank the Lord that neither of us were hurt.

Drug addicts will do anything to support their habit. They will steal from their friends and family. They will lie, cheat, and double-cross without giving it a second thought.

Most of the guys I hung around with at the time would shoot drugs intramuscular into their legs, which often led to gangrene. Their flesh would rot as it hung on their bodies, and it smelled horrid. Some lost their legs this way. Once I told a man he couldn't stay in my apartment any longer. He was lying on the floor after a long night of partying. I entered the room, walked up to him, pointed my finger in his face, and told him to leave immediately. At that moment, he grabbed a sword with a 36-inch blade and jabbed it under my armpit. The point of the sword penetrated all the way to my lung. Blood spurted from the wound, covering the floor in a growing red puddle. A friend helped me to his car and drove as fast as he could to the emergency room.

The doctors immediately recognized that I had a collapsed lung. I could even hear the air rushing out of the punctured lung. The sword had missed my heart by about 1/8 of an inch. If it had traveled that tiny bit more, I would have died that night. Once again, the Angels had intervened so I could live to see the day I could truly accept God's help and go into recovery. I have also learned that the important thing is not how long you live but whether you live for Christ.

I did not press charges against the man who stabbed me, but I probably should have. For a long time, I knew that if I came across him, I would have sought revenge with at least a swift kick in the groin. Years later, in an Alcoholics Anonymous meeting, I realized I needed to forgive him, which I did.

I spent 10 days in the hospital recovering and healing from the collapsed lung.

My days in the 3-bedroom apartment were bound to come to an end. One day the Sheriff knocked on the door and told me I had three days to vacate the premises. It was gut-wrenching news. Being kicked to the street again felt like another colossal failure.

I had no car at the time. I had a TV, a bed, some couches and some other furniture – none of which I could take with me. I abandoned all that in the apartment and left with a full backpack and the clothes I was wearing. It was another all-time low for me. I couldn't believe I had lost everything yet again.

Included in "everything" were my self-respect, self-worth, and relationship with God. I lost things in storage, including family heirlooms and objects I had saved from my childhood. Among the heirlooms was my mother's wedding ring, the loss of which cut deep into my already wounded heart.

The most tragic loss was, of course, the relationship with my children. As with my friends and extended family, I had disrespected them, stolen from them, and abandoned them. Everything was about me, my fears, and my addictions. I can never take those things back. Hopefully, my family will read these words ... and when they do, I want them to know how sorry I am for how I chose to live my life. I love each one of you. To my kids, Tangela and Loren Jr. - I love you two so much, and I'm so sorry that the things I did in my life hurt you the way they did. No child deserves to be treated that way. From the bottom of my heart, I'm sorry. There's truly something to be said about living amends by the Grace. I love you both very, very much.

After leaving the apartment, with nowhere to go or live, God stayed with me. He was knocking on the door of my heart, but I was not listening. I was not yet ready to commit my life to Christ. Apparently, I hadn't had enough. The warning signs were everywhere around me. I needed to get clean.

The Bible says we are to be good stewards in this life. Indeed, I am writing this book to be a good steward and tell my story of hope and faith. I desire to continue to live my life in a meaningful and productive way for God. I want to leave a lasting legacy, especially for my children, stepchildren, and grandchildren.

Deuteronomy 31:6: "The Lord your God will go with you. He will never leave you. He'll never desert you."

Psalm 107:6: "Then they cried out to the Lord in their trouble, and he delivered them from their distress."

It is never too late to change direction, place your trust in God, and ask Him for guidance. Committing my life to Christ was the single most important decision I have ever made. It allowed me to have the riches I now enjoy: being clean and sober, marrying my best friend, having kids and grandkids, and living in the Light of Jesus rather than the darkness of addictions and the poor life choices that come with them. God has been immensely good to me.

Titus 3:3-8: "At one time we too were foolish, disobedient, deceived and enslaved by all kinds of passions and pleasures. We lived in malice and envy, being hated and hating one another. But when the kindness and love of God our Savior appeared, he saved us, not because of righteous things we had done, but because of His mercy. He saved us through the washing of rebirth and renewal by the Holy Spirit, whom He poured out on us generously through Jesus Christ our Savior, so that, having been justified by His grace, we might become heirs having the hope of eternal life. This is a trustworthy saying. And I want you to stress these things, so that those who have trusted in God may be careful to devote themselves to doing what is good. These things are excellent and profitable for everyone."

Chapter 6

Flesh and Blood

**"Here is what people who belong to this world do.
They try to satisfy what their sinful desires want
to do. They long for what their sinful eyes look at.
They take pride in what they have and they do.
All of this comes from the world.
None of it comes from the Father."
1 John 2:16**

Someone once told me that every time an addict puts drugs into their body, the demon inside of them gets loaded. I never understood that until I got clean. Addiction and alcoholism go hand-in-hand with spiritual warfare. You can call it demon possession or something else, but this is what happens.

Our materialistic society invites addiction through the front door. It gives us every opportunity to sink into the cesspool of drugs, alcohol, lust, lies, deceit, theft, despair, and hopelessness. No matter how hard I tried, I could not break the vicious cycle. Once I was up to my neck in the cesspool, there were only three possible ways out: rescue, jail, or death.

I came close to death more times than I care to recall. By the grace of God, my Lord and Savior, I lived. And for this, I give thanks.

God makes over 7,000 promises to humankind in the Bible. One of them, **Proverbs 3:26**, says, "For the Lord will be at your side and will keep your foot from being snared."

My risky lifestyle of flesh and blood was unrelenting, painful, and empty. I filled the void with cigarettes, alcohol, drugs, and sex. I had sex with many, many women. I would often meet a girl and think she was "the one". We would go on a date and then have sex right away. This was lust, leading me blindly towards more poor choices. The One I was looking for was of Spirit, not of the flesh. But I didn't know that yet. And I was extremely fortunate that I never caught any sexually transmitted diseases.

In a sense, every unhealthy, broken sexual encounter I ever had has helped mold me into the man I am. That is true of all of my poor choices. I am a man of God. I am not perfect. Deep down inside every broken person, I believe there is a lost little child yearning to know how much God loves them. I firmly believe that absolutely nothing happens by mistake in God's world.

There was a time when I was married to Sharon, the mother of my children. After Sharon and I divorced, I was in and out of relationships. Nobody quite seemed to be "the one". For a brief time after our divorce, I was clean. It did not last long.

But when a person's lifestyle revolves around drugs and alcohol, they justify having sex outside of the marriage covenant.

Today, I am happily married to my best friend, Teresa. This is by far the healthiest relationship I have ever had. Teresa is the love of my life.

Psalm 40:
I waited patiently for the Lord
    he turned to me and heard my cry.
He lifted me out of the slimy pit,
    out of the mud and mire;
He set my feet on a rock
    and gave me a firm place to stand.

He put a new song in my mouth,
a hymn of praise to our God.
Many will see and fear the Lord
and put their trust in him.
Blessed is the one
who trusts in the Lord,
who does not look to the proud,
to those who turn aside to false gods.
Many, Lord my God,
are the wonders you have done,
the things you planned for us.
None can compare with you;
were I to speak and tell of your deeds,
they would be too many to declare.
Sacrifice and offering you did not desire—
but my ears you have opened—
burnt offerings and sin offerings you did not require.
Then I said, "Here I am, I have come—
it is written about me in the scroll.
I desire to do your will, my God;
your law is within my heart."
I proclaim your saving acts in the great assembly;
I do not seal my lips, Lord,
as you know.
I do not hide your righteousness in my heart;
I speak of your faithfulness and your saving help.
I do not conceal your love and your faithfulness
from the great assembly.
Do not withhold your mercy from me, Lord;

may your love and faithfulness always protect me.
For troubles without number surround me;
   my sins have overtaken me, and I cannot see.
They are more than the hairs of my head,
   and my heart fails within me.
Be pleased to save me, Lord;
   come quickly, Lord, to help me.
May all who want to take my life
   be put to shame and confusion;
may all who desire my ruin
   be turned back in disgrace.
May those who say to me, "Aha! Aha!"
   be appalled at their own shame.
But may all who seek you
   rejoice and be glad in you;
may those who long for your saving help always say,
   "The Lord is great!"
But as for me, I am poor and needy;
   may the Lord think of me.
You are my help and my deliverer;
   you are my God, do not delay.

That says so much.

I do not have many regrets. There are certain things I wish I had not done. However, the choices I made, be they good or bad, have allowed me to become a better person, husband, father, grandfather, and friend. And most importantly, a better child of God.

God was always calling me.

I would run across verses like **Isaiah 45:22-23**: "Turn to me and be saved, all you ends of the earth; for I am God, and there is no other. By myself I have sworn, my mouth has uttered in all integrity a word that will not be revoked: Before me every knee will bow; by me every tongue will swear."

God was seeking me all my life.

Whether I was chasing down another high or one-night stand, I always felt empty inside. I lived in a constant state of guilt and shame. I often didn't care if I lived or died. I could not understand the simple verse of **Matthew 6:33**: "But put God's kingdom first. Do what he wants you to do. Then all those things will also be given to you." **Matthew 6:34**: "So don't worry about tomorrow. Tomorrow will worry about itself. Each day has enough trouble of its own." I am alive today because of my Lord and Savior, Jesus Christ.

When another person says they love you, it is based upon your relationship up to that point. When God says he loves you, it is eternal and based upon everything you have ever done and will do, be it good or bad.

When you are so far gone as I was, you begin to believe your own lies. I would talk about getting clean, but I wouldn't. I would tell people I would be there for them, but I would be absent when their time of need came. Notice that I referred to them as "people" and not as "friends". You have no real friends when you are using. As soon as the dope and the money are gone, so are they. So was I.

I worried about things I had no control over while neglecting the things I could change. Through pain, suffering, and heartache, I have learned that God will never make me do anything, but He will undoubtedly make me wish I had. The road I chose was filled with darkness and despair.

Proverbs 16:5: "The Lord detests all the proud of heart. Be sure of this: They will not go unpunished."

That is why we cannot serve Jesus while clinging to our self-importance. When we give Him second place in our lives, the work of the Holy Spirit is hindered. When I focused on myself and not on Him, I made foolish mistakes. The key to overcoming my pride was to focus my eyes on God. The depth of His character and He alone is worthy of my praise – nothing else.

The detox community knew me well. If they gave frequent flyer miles for going to detox, I would have been in the Million-Mile Club. I even committed myself to two lock-down treatment centers. The commitment I needed to make was to Jesus.

Chapter 7

Getting Clean

"At one time we too were foolish, disobedient, deceived and enslaved by all kinds of passions and pleasures. We lived in malice and envy, being hated and hating one another. But when the kindness and love of God our Savior appeared, he saved us, not because of righteous things we had done, but because of his mercy. He saved us through the washing of rebirth and renewal by the Holy Spirit, whom he poured out on us generously through Jesus Christ our Savior, so that, having been justified by his grace, we might become heirs having the hope of eternal life. This is a trustworthy saying. And I want you to stress these things, so that those who have trusted in God may be careful to devote themselves to doing what is good. These things are excellent and profitable for everyone."
Titus 3:3-8

In Luke 15:11-32, Jesus tells the Parable of the Prodigal Son. In it, there are two sons of a wealthy man. The younger son asks their father for his inheritance. His father grants the wish, and the son squanders the money and ends up destitute. He returns home and begs his father to let him be his servant. To the son's surprise, the father not only rejects the idea but lovingly welcomes him back and throws a celebration in his honor. The older brother is jealous and does not attend the festivities. The father says the older brother should be happy for his younger brother, not resentful.

The lesson is that God loves us even as we sin, and when we repent, He will forgive us and welcome us back with open arms. I see my own life of addiction, crime, lies, and other sins as the Prodigal Son on steroids.

You may not realize or recognize His presence, but it is always there. Sometimes, God will intervene, and you just need to recognize the chance for a course change and redemption.

In late 2004, I was homeless, and my girlfriend and I lived in my Buick Skylark. We were living hard and running ragged. I was ravaged by addiction, pain, and self-pity.

Psalm 37:4: "Find your delight in the Lord. Then he will give you everything your heart really wants."

On Halloween night of that year, God showed me that I did not have to live that way anymore. I remember every detail as vividly as if it happened yesterday.

It was a cold, foggy evening with a gentle breeze – typical weather for late October in Northwest Washington. I had spent the day hustling and panhandling to get enough cash to buy my daily fix, leaving $5 for gas money. After I bought the drugs, I returned to my car to relax. Some kids came out of the bushes and threw eggs at my car. When I realized what was happening, I started my car and chased them down, almost running one of them over. I spent the next few hours driving around Bellingham.

My girlfriend and I decided to spend the night in a parking lot above the Cornwall Church, a Christian church in Bellingham affiliated with the Church of God Movement. It was in a relatively unpopulated rural area between Bellingham and Ferndale. I knew the lot would be secure as it was blocked off by a cable, which you could lift and drive underneath. The church was built on a hill, and the upper parking lot overlooked the entire area, so I could see if anyone was approaching. It was also hidden from the road, so nobody driving by would know I was there. My main concern, of course, was being seen by the cops.

That night as we fell asleep in the backseat of my car, the chains of addiction wrapped tight around my body, mind, and spirit, I cried out to Jesus. I prayed to be liberated from my addictions and destructive lifestyle. On some level, I recognized that every big mistake I had ever made was a direct result of drugs, alcohol, or some toxic behavior. "Dear Lord, please get us out of this way of life. I can't take it anymore! I've had enough, and I'm sick and tired of being sick and tired."

Suddenly, an overwhelming sense of peace came over me, a feeling that had eluded me for a long time. At the moment, I did not fully understand what was happening or why.

The time would soon come to break the chains that had held me for so long. My long road to recovery began at that moment. I did not believe I could live differently, and I did not trust Jesus yet. But better days would come soon enough. That night I asked the Lord to help us get out of the destructive lives we were living. God works in mysterious ways, and you often get what you pray for – just not the way you expect it. One day I would even lead recovery groups at that very same church.

The next day, on November 1st, we decided to stay in a run-down local motel instead of my car. I really wanted to take a shower and get a good night's sleep. Also, it was late autumn, and the weather outside was getting cold. I slept really well that night.

The following day around 8:00 AM, we left to buy heroin and crack. My dealer was out of crack, so we just bought some heroin and returned to the motel. Driving back, we passed a county sheriff who was just finishing writing an infraction to someone in a car beside the road. The officer pulled us over, too.

When I rolled down my window, he yelled at me, calling me Donnie Parker. To this day, I have no idea who Donnie Parker is. My girlfriend yelled back, "No, that's Loren McWilliams!"

We both exited our cars and met between them. "Do you have any warrants out for your arrest, Mr. McWilliams?" the cop asked.

"As a matter of fact, I do," I responded honestly. I indeed had a few misdemeanor warrants.

The sheriff decided to search me. I put the heroin in a pocket in my sweatshirt. At first I thought he would miss it ... but then he put his hand in my pocket and pulled it out. He asked if it was mine or hers. Of course, I told him it belonged to me. And with that statement, my old drug world would begin to fall apart. Little did I know at that moment that I would soon become a whole new man.

I spent the next 38 days locked up in the Whatcom County Jail and going through withdrawal from my heroin addiction. It was the worst I had ever felt in my life. Every cell of my body revolted against me, and I was in a constant state of panic and anxiety. By the grace of God, I hope I never feel anything like that ever again. I barely slept the entire 38 days, and when I did, it was not sound sleep. They put me into a program called Whatcom County Drug Court, and the court sent me into a treatment program.

At first I was hopeful that someone would bail me out. However, I really didn't have any family at the time because they had all kicked me out of their lives. My friends were all drug addicts who spent every penny they had on their own addictions. Not even my girlfriend could come up with the measly $100 to get me out of jail. In fact, she was able to access my bank account, so she withdrew all my money to support her drug habit.

In the end, staying locked up was for the best. Kicking heroin was a necessary step on my road to recovery, and being in jail gave me no choice but to suffer through the withdrawal.

I shared my jail cell with eight other guys. I knew several of them, and two of them were also believers. They laid hands on me to calm me down as I went through withdrawal.

There were only two people that would even talk to me. One was my nephew, Brian, and the other was the pastor from my church, Steve Schroeder. Pastor Steve did come to visit me once while I was in jail. I asked him to bail me out as well. He said no. He told me that God put me there for a reason and that if I didn't get it right this time, I was destined to repeat it over and over until I either got it right or died.

On December 10, 2004, I entered rehab at American Behavioral Health Systems (ABHS) across the state in Spokane. I stayed there until March 10, 2005. When I left Whatcom County after going through withdrawal, my skin was pale and white like marble but without the warmth. I barely weighed 120 lbs.

It felt amazing to finally be free of my addictions. I had a lot of fun in early recovery, and I made some great friends at ABHS. For the first time in my life, I stopped fighting everything and everyone. The flicker of hope that had almost been extinguished within me began to return. I was starting to truly live again, and flourish!

I remember going to a one-on-one with my counselor at ABHS. I started running my mouth, going on about drugs, my girlfriend, partying, and my generally toxic lifestyle. The counselor looked me directly in the eyes and said, "Liar." I was taken aback – had he just called me a liar? "Liar," he repeated. I felt crushed! However, the point he was trying to make was 100% true. The life I had been living to that point was based on lies and deceit. When that sunk it, it was a huge turning point in my recovery.

There were 65 people that had been sent to ABHS from Whatcom County Drug Court. Of that number, only two of us stayed clean long-term – a guy named Jonathan and me. I had gone to school with Jonathan's mother, so we had one connection besides our recovery. I know that many of the other 63 who did relapse would get clean later. Sometimes it takes many attempts at recovery to make it permanent.

The rehab facility found out I had owned a janitorial business, so they put me in charge of the chore list. Everyone in rehab was supposed to work, so I got to tell them what to do, which I enjoyed. I rotated the jobs on the chore list, so nobody got stuck doing the same thing every day. That responsibility gave me a sense of self-worth in my early recovery.

After 30 days in rehab at AHBS, you can go into Phase Two, which is called Recovery House. During this phase, you can sign out of the center for activities such as going to the YMCA or an AA meeting. It was at this point that I truly learned to have fun again. Life felt full, abundant, and worth living.

One time my friend Vato and I took a bus to downtown Spokane. We were always goofing around and having fun. While walking down the sidewalk, I tripped and fell, scraping both my knees. Vato looked down and asked me, "Are you done?"

"Done with what?" I asked.

"You know. Done with this way of life. Using drugs and all that."

I thought about it for a moment, thinking about my answer. "Yes," I said, "I believe I am." That day I made a commitment to Christ to stay clean. And I have kept that commitment!

Colossians 1:13-14: "God rescued us from dead-end alleys and dark dungeons. He's set us up in the kingdom of the Son he loves so much, the Son who got us out of the pit we were in, got rid of the sins we were doomed to keep repeating."

Vato and I had some good times at ABHS. Whenever someone graduated from the program, we all sat in a circle and had to say something positive about the person. Mostly people repeated some mumbo-jumbo you could read in any generic self-help book. For Vato and me, these graduation circles became an opportunity for fun and laughter. Sometimes I would laugh so hard that my stomach and face hurt. The counselor who led the sessions was into New Age jargon. She would say things like, "I put pink elephants in your rock," or "May white pillowy soft clouds envelop you." How can you not laugh at statements like that? Also, who the heck can say that kind of stuff and maintain a straight face?

Sometimes, Vato and I would get in trouble for laughing too much. We were literally sent to the office for having too much fun. Being called to the office for disciplinary matters felt more like junior high than the world of mature adults, the irony of which only added to the absurd comedy that gave us so much entertainment.

Of the months and years I've spent in prisons and rehab centers, laughter has often been one of the things that helped me get through without completely losing my mind. Laughter in such dark and serious places stands in stark contrast to the way people are expected to behave there. I've lost count of the number of times people have complained or reported me for expressing my sense of humor. But if you're already in jail, what have you got to lose?

Proverbs 27:17: "Iron sharpens iron, and one person sharpens the wits of another."

Life is too short and precious to spend time being miserable. If one can find humor in a situation, the moment should be savored with a good hearty laugh.

45 days into the recovery program at ABHS, a brown recluse spider bit me on the bottom of my nose. It made me quite ill, which was awful but also a blessing as it did get me restricted to bed so I could rest. And man, did I need to rest!

My nose swelled up from the bite, and I began to resemble a deformed Donald Duck. It was pretty hideous. The bite took a few weeks to heal, but I no longer looked like a contorted duck once it did.

While I was in rehab, I found out that my girlfriend was using my car, living with a drug dealer, and still living the destructive lifestyle we had shared. Besides taking my money and car, she sold off as many of my possessions as she could get her hands on. I was glad to be so far away from her and those kinds of patterns. I wasn't happy about losing my things, but I was truly healing and entering a new phase of my life, so on balance, things were going in the right direction.

Part of the requirements of drug court was that when I finished rehab, I had to continue with the four phases of their program.

Phase One was to be verified clean and sober for at least 30 days, have no court sanctions for 30 days, attend weekly court hearings, and submit to urine testing three times per week.

Phase Two was to attend two 12- Step meetings every week, submit to random drug tests, attend biweekly court hearings, and complete 60 days clean and sober without jail sanctions.

Phase Three was to appear in court every three weeks, submit to random drug tests, obtain a 12- Step sponsor, and complete at least 60 days clean and sober without jail sanctions.

Phase Four was to appear in court every four weeks, submit to random drug tests, do community service, and either get a job or enroll in school.

I told the court that I fully intended to do the four phases of the program, but I was lying. Instead, I planned to take the bus back to Bellingham, then go to Port Townsend on the Olympic Peninsula where my so-called girlfriend was living. She had my car and my few remaining possessions. She was also dating someone else by then, but I figured she would get back with me when she saw me.

As the Greyhound bus crossed the Cascade Mountains at Snoqualmie Pass heading toward Bellingham, I distinctly heard and felt the Holy Spirit tell me that I needed to go back to Bellingham and do the right thing – meaning finishing the program. I thought the four-phase program was stupid, and I argued with the Holy Spirit for about an hour on that bus ride. As was my pattern, the last thing I wanted to do was the "right thing".

God was very clear that if I wished to have a life worth living, I had to make some hard choices moving forward. I would need to remain clean and stay away from the toxic relationship with my girlfriend. I had urged her to get clean before, but she strongly resisted going down that path. I've learned the hard way that you can only get clean and stay clean for yourself; you can't do it for another person.

By the Grace of God, I did return to Bellingham and completed the program. I finished it 13 months later – on January 13, 2005. Most people in the program who had started before me were still there. Many took two or even four years to accomplish what I did in just over a year. I wasn't messing around. It was the first real accomplishment of my life. The only things I had finished up to that point were jail sentences.

It felt great to know I could accomplish something positive in my life. It was a massive victory for me. It also taught me I could learn to stay clean under trying circumstances.

When I arrived back in Bellingham, I had $1,000 to my name and no place to live. As I walked to a Narcotics Anonymous (NA) meeting on that first day back in town, I looked up and saw my girlfriend driving my car. Seated beside her and in the back seat were other drug addicts. She pulled up, and all she could say was, "Hey, can I get some money?"

I was surprised she had the audacity to ask me for money after she had already emptied my bank account and stolen every one of my possessions of value she could get her hands on, including my car. "I'd like my car back," was my response. She drove away.

Our interaction strengthened my resolve to go to the NA meeting. I knew that setting a precedent on that first day would be an essential step in my recovery.

I had no idea where I would lay my head that night. I had burned every bridge. Fortunately, a friend met me after the NA meeting and took me to a clean and sober house. The house was actually a scam run by a lady named Pam. I lived in the Pam-scam house for about two months. It was at least a roof over my head and was compliant with drug court.

From the first time I set foot in Pam's house, I didn't care for the place. The house had terrible energy, and it made me feel uneasy. When a roommate asked if I wanted a tarot card reading, my suspicions were confirmed. It was not a healthy place to be! The spiritual warfare in that house was off the chart.

After a few more weeks in the house, I uncovered more of the darkness there. The house manager and one of the guys from drug court were doing heroin together. Since I was clean, they wanted me out and accused me of stealing a pair of socks.

In the second month, Pam allowed me to pay rent a couple of days late, then kicked me out for paying the rent late but did not refund the money. To this day, Pam continues to take advantage of people trying to recover from drug addiction and rebuild their lives. She allows addicts to move in, takes their money, then finds trivial reasons to kick them out.

As usual, God was looking out for me, and I got a room at Oxford House, an honestly-run place operated by caring people. It was much nicer than Pam's place. It housed up to eight people in recovery, and several of the guys who lived there I already knew from drug court.

There are almost 3,000 Oxford Houses throughout the United States and the world. They are self-supported and self-run and operate on a not-for-profit model. The focus is on recovery, sobriety, abstinence, and self-sufficiency. They are run as democracies and do not have a "staff", as the occupants are in charge of every aspect of the operation. For example, in our house, we held positions for three months. Those positions included the President, Treasurer, and

House Comptroller. Expenses were shared equally. We had mandatory weekly business meetings. Attendance at recovery meetings was also obligatory. Anyone caught using drugs or alcohol was given a half hour to gather their stuff and move out. They weren't messing around!

To get admitted to Oxford house, you were put through an arduous interview process, after which you had to have 80% of the occupants vote in your favor. Since eight people lived there, it required six votes. Because the others liked my leadership style, they repeatedly voted me in as President.

I lived in Oxford House for about two and a half years between 2005 and 2007. While there, I learned to have fun and laugh more. I really got my act together. It was the first time in my life I had ever kept current on my bills, which was a big lesson. It was a healing place to be. I attended recovery meetings every day, found a sponsor, and worked the 12 Steps to freedom and recovery. I attended church regularly and felt a joy and ease in my life I hadn't known since childhood. I made amends with my family and friends who I had hurt during my decades as an addict. My son and daughter had suffered the most, which felt devastating. Making amends to them was my highest priority.

When someone gets clean and the healing process begins, things come to the surface you need to deal with. For example, I had never grieved the loss of my parents. When my mother died, I took a lot of pain pills to avoid feeling my emotions. I finally began to grieve from my heart and release the shame I carried for how my life turned out.

I also learned that one of my spiritual gifts was sensing whenever anyone would bring drugs or alcohol into the house. It would even wake me up out of a deep sleep at 3 AM if someone came into the house with drugs or under the influence.

I met some of my dearest friends at Oxford House, and over a decade later many of these wonderful people remain my closest friends, a testament to the value of both the difficult and joyful experiences and true brotherly love we shared then and continue to share to this day. I lived at Oxford House so long they started calling me The Godfather. I took that as a sign that it was time to move on, and so I did. God has put some amazing people in my life over the years!

My life of crime, addiction, and constantly being sent to jail was finally coming to a halt. By the Grace of God, my past began to remind me rather than define me. The black cloud that always seemed to follow me around was dissipating.

Proverbs 4:25-27: "Let your eyes look straight ahead, fix your gaze directly before you. Give careful thought to the paths for your feet and be steadfast in all your ways. Do not turn to the right or the left; keep your foot from evil."

I'm going to go out on a limb here and share my two-part theory of addiction. First, I believe that it is in our nature to sin. It was my sinful nature that kept me repeating crimes, getting drunk and high, and making other terrible life choices. Living a life of sin guarantees suffering and can easily lead to premature death. In this way, addiction is a disease of the spirit.

Second, addiction is a disease with its own bodily causes, treatments, and cures. It is a cunning, powerful, and potentially deadly disease that I endured for most of my life. In this way, addiction is a disease of the body.

The disease of addiction can kill you just as one's sinful lifestyle can. Surrendering my life to Jesus Christ, as I finally did on November 2, 2004, no doubt saved my life. That's when I finally fully stopped the insanity of drugs and alcohol.

There were so many times before that day when my addictions could have killed me. Once clean, I no longer needed to look over my shoulder. I learned to be unashamed of who I am. I am a New Creation in Christ!

There are a million little things that eat away at you as an addict: the fear of arrest, actually being arrested, the court dates, the fines, the holds on your driver's license when you don't pay those fines, the jail time, and the list goes on and on. Once in recovery, those weights are all lifted from your shoulders. You no longer need to beg, borrow, steal, lie, cheat, and betray your friends and family to get your next fix. You are no longer at war with God, for you are finally at peace.

Deuteronomy 4:9: "Only be careful, and watch yourselves closely so that you do not forget the things your eyes have seen or let them fade from your heart as long as you live. Teach them to your children and to their children after them."

As I write these words, I have been clean for 16 years. My soul has grown, and I no longer doubt God's goodness. I am grateful that God will continue to be with me for all of the days of my life here on Earth and through all eternity. For most of my life, I lived with an inner conflict between good and evil. Every day I was being called, but I did not recognize it. What a person chooses to do with this conflict will determine the kind of change and growth they will experience.

Before I recommitted my life to Jesus in recovery, I only knew toxic relationships.

John 10:10: "A thief comes only to steal and kill and destroy. I have come so they may have life. I want them to have it in the fullest possible way."

There are many moments of my past that feel as if they were part of a terrible movie. But by the Grace of our Lord and Savior, that part of my life has become a story of redemption, grace, love, and forgiveness. During my years of addiction, I never cared for anyone but myself. I lived to use, and I used to live. My days of living life like a ghost are now fading into the past. I now seek to stay healthy and loving toward my own life, support others in recovery, pay it forward, and try to share a little bit of happiness everywhere I go.

Romans 8:28: "We know that in all things God works for the good of those who love Him. He appointed them to be saved in keeping with His purpose."

Life continues to unfold with triumphs and misfortunes, births and deaths, joy and suffering, and all the dramas that we experience living life among God's creation. I wish I could say that becoming clean and sober meant no longer enduring hardship and heartbreak. That is not the case. But I do move through the storms with a calmness and faith that can only come by surrendering one's life to God.

1 Peter 5:8: "Be watchful and control yourselves. Your enemy the devil is like a roaring lion. He prowls around looking for someone to swallow up."

In early November, 2007, a series of tragedies and misfortunes happened in my life. This came at a time when I was celebrating three years of being clean. They say things happen in threes, but in this case, five traumatic events took place within three weeks. First, my fiance broke up with me. Then my former brother-in-law died from an alcohol and heroin overdose. Then two more deaths – my uncle and then a gentleman I had been mentoring.

The fifth occurred on November 20, 2007. I was on my way to an AA meeting when I had an overwhelming feeling that my daughter was dying. I had never felt anything like this before. My daughter, Tangela, was full-term pregnant with a baby girl. Within 10 minutes of my premonition, she called to tell me there was something wrong with the baby. At the time, I was in the process of moving to Redmond, Oregon, where she and her husband lived with their first child.

The baby hadn't moved in three days. She was rushed to the hospital for an emergency C-section. The baby had lost all its blood. The blood, having nowhere else to go, entered my daughter. To this day, nobody knows why or what happened. My daughter survived the ordeal; her baby, Willow, did not. It was a terrible tragedy. I do find some solace knowing that I will meet Willow in heaven one day. My heart still grieves my daughter's loss. I find comfort in Jesus and Him alone.

Chapter 8

The Church

**"And let us not give up meeting together. Some
are in the habit of doing this. Instead, let us
encourage one another with words of hope.
Let us do this even more as you see
Christ's return approaching."
Hebrews 10:25**

I believe as a part of the church in the Kingdom of God. I
believe beyond a shadow of a doubt that we are meant for
community.

I think we could do better as a family of God within the body
of believers. I don't say this to denigrate the church but to
elevate it.

In my teens, I would often attend church with my mother.
We were both close to the pastor there. I remember crying
out many times, telling them I had a drug problem and that I
was desperate to find a way out. I did not know where else to
turn. I was not asking them to fix me; I wanted some love and
compassion. Each time I broached the subject of addiction,
they would sweep it under the rug and explain why it was
unacceptable to bring such problems into the church. I found
this ironic because Jesus would hang out with broken people
like me.

I do not fault the church or anyone else for my poor choices.
But I think churches drop the ball repeatedly when it comes
to addressing uncomfortable topics like addiction. Churches
often lack the tools of compassion and Grace when it comes to
addicts. It's not like substance abuse and addiction are new;

they have been around since at least as far back as when man learned to ferment grapes.

After 11 years of sobriety, I returned to the church I had attended with my mother. It had probably been 20 years since I stepped foot inside. The people in the congregation had aged, but they were as rude to me upon my return as they had been decades ago when I was a drug-addicted teenager looking for help. It saddened me to see the body of Christ act in ways that contradict His teachings. This isn't to say I am without fault. We can all continue to learn to be more loving and compassionate. And we can all learn to forgive.

Christ did not come for the wealthy and comfortable; he came for the sick, afflicted, and downtrodden. The Bible says we are to be the hands and feet of Jesus. In my experience, many churches don't have a clue when it comes to dealing with addicts and addictions. This is true of the church I currently attend. I have given testimony several times before our church, and I think it has helped people see what is happening in their midst.

Recently, my partner and I were looking for a suitable local church to start a faith-based recovery group. One pastor said to me that my "type" was not welcome in his church and that they didn't have any unsaved people in their congregation. I get that most people who go to church are saved. But the teachings of Jesus go far beyond that. I'm sure there were people in his flock that were suffering through addictions and needed to come out of the closet so they could be helped. Addiction is rampant in our society and touches every community. To think it is something that only happens "elsewhere" is to be in deep denial of a grave issue that ruins lives, families and friendships, and tears at the seams of every town and city.

One of the reasons I am writing this book is to help familiarize the church with the issue of addiction and assist in creating more faith-based recovery groups. It would be immensely helpful if addicts simply knew there were faith-based groups ready to welcome them with open arms any time they are ready. There are only two such recovery groups in Whatcom County, and ours is one of them. And that's in a population of around 230,000 people! There are Alcoholics Anonymous (AA), Narcotics Anonymous (NA), Cocaine Anonymous (CA), Marijuana Anonymous (MA), Porn Addicts Anonymous (PAA), Gamblers Anonymous (GA), and other such groups. But there are very few safe Christian recovery groups.

Isaiah 61:1: "The Spirit of the Lord and King is on me. The Lord has anointed me to announce good news to poor people. He has sent me to comfort those whose hearts have been broken. He has sent me to announce freedom for those who have been captured. He wants me to set prisoners free from their dark cells."

There are times when a person comes along and is serious about wanting help with their addiction. We, as the body of Christ, should point them in the direction of that help. I believe that churches should play a significant role in addressing addiction. I think churches should allocate as much funding as they can for recovery programs and other things that would genuinely help their congregation and community. There does not need to be a recovery center in every church, but there should be far more than exist now. The need is great. There are so many people, especially former addicts and the people who love them, who are willing and able to put in the time, work, and even money to bring such programs to fruition. My partner and I are two such people.

Drug abuse has been rising for decades and shows no signs of abating. Each year in the United States alone, around 53 million people 12 and older use illegal drugs or abuse prescription drugs. That's nearly 20% of the population! If you include tobacco and alcohol, those numbers rise to 160 million people, or a little over 60% of this population. Around 25% of people with drug addiction use opioids. If you broaden the group to include those addicted to gambling (two million), pornography (200,000), sex (12-30 million), overeating (5% of the population), and other addictions, then we're talking about 210 million Americans! And of those who are afflicted with addiction, less than 10% receive treatment. Do you know what is in every single community in the country? Churches!

Even those who don't suffer from addiction are affected by it, directly or indirectly. It destroys every kind of relationship and degrades every community, religious or not. As the body of Christ, we should do so much more to reach out to the addicted with love, acceptance, forgiveness, and recovery programs.

So what can each of us do to help?

First, we all need to pray for the broken-hearted in and around our neighborhoods, schools, community events, etc. – anywhere and everywhere you can pray, please do so. Talk to your pastors, elders, or deacons. Consider starting a faith-based recovery group. If you don't know where one is or want assistance in creating one, please reach out to us. Our contact information is at the end of this book.

Although my story involves coming into recovery from several 12-Step support groups, at this point in my recovery I lean more toward faith-based groups. A person must be willing to go to any lengths to get and stay clean!

I lead a Christian recovery group called The Most Excellent Way at the Northwest Baptist Church in Bellingham, Washington. We meet Wednesday nights at 6 PM. We have a small core group of five or six people who meet regularly. A few years ago, when we were at one of the mega-churches in our county, we averaged around 30 people at each meeting.

There is so much to do beyond praying and starting more groups. We can become informed and educated on addiction and recovery issues and bring the topic to the forefront of conversations and the news. We can reach out to the afflicted. They need to know they are wanted and loved and that God loves them unconditionally.

Addicts like me have sinned against God and broken His laws. We have disobeyed Him, and yet He still wants us to come boldly back to the throne of Grace. He wants us to go to Him, and He wants to put His arms around us and tell us how much He loves us. He is the almighty God – the enduring creator of the universe. He is interested in each one of us, even those who are strung out junkies and broken beyond measure. He would have died just for me, even if I was the only person who ever lived. God loves us all with an everlasting love.

Jeremiah 31:3: "The Lord appeared to us in the past. He said, 'I have loved you with a love that lasts forever. I have kept on loving you with a kindness that never fails.'"

Every addict has had the hopeless feeling of not feeling that they belong, especially to a church. Most feel so ashamed and guilty that they do not realize they are worthy of God's love.

Isaiah 43 1-4: "But now, this is what the Lord says—he who created you, Jacob, he who formed you, Israel: 'Do not fear, for I have redeemed you; I have summoned you by name; you are mine. When you pass through the waters, I will be with you; and when you pass through the rivers, they will not sweep over you. When you walk through the fire, you will not be burned; the flames will not set you ablaze. For I am the Lord your God, the Holy One of Israel, your Savior; I give Egypt for your ransom, Cush and Seba in your stead. Since you are precious and honored in my sight, and because I love you, I will give people in exchange for you, nations in exchange for your life.'"

Psalms 147:3 tells us that the Father faithfully heals the brokenhearted and binds their wounds. The power to mend brokenness is found in seeking and spending time with the Lord and seeing ourselves through Christ's eyes. May we all be reminded that those who are addicted need the church and the family of God to surround and love them. Each of us long to know that we matter - especially to God. But we need each other, too. We all desire to be loved without judgment.

John 3:16: "God so loved the world that he gave his one and only Son. Anyone who believes in Him will not die but will have eternal life."

Jesus came for the brokenhearted. He even said to the thief on the Cross that "You will be with me in paradise." (Luke 23:43)

We all need to be loving, accepting, and forgiving of others for who they are, not what they have or have not done in the past.

I am still broken, just not as broken as when I was homeless, drug-addicted, and living in my car. I don't have a monopoly on recovery. By the grace of God, I am alive, free, and clean. I now know that it takes a whole Bible to make me a whole believer.

Most churches shun people with addictions and certain diseases such as Hepatitis C and AIDS. There is an underlying belief that you deserve your suffering, that it is God's punishment. This kind of thinking goes against everything Jesus taught us. He wants us to be compassionate toward ALL people.

The last thing an addict needs or wants is for us to heap more guilt and shame on them. We have already done that to ourselves. We have a backlog of regrets that haunt our dreams. Besides my own experience, I have mentored many others to know that this is the case.

Let us approach the addicted with love and mercy. Not all want help now, but we can be there for those who are ready. We can pray. We can steer them in the right direction. Ultimately, it is up to them to seek help.

I believe there are five stages to recovery:

Stage #1 – Heal physically

Stage #2 – Heal mentally

Stage #3 – Heal emotionally

Stage #4 – Heal spiritually

Stage #5 – Restoration

Stage 5 is the most important. Many people skip one or more stages, focusing on the earlier ones and ignoring the later ones.

Some pastors are naïve and have been taken advantage of by addicts and alcoholics. As a result, they may have difficulty trusting that they sincerely want to get clean and sober. It can indeed be challenging to distinguish between those who are pulling a hustle and those who sincerely want to get clean and sober. Acquiring the skill of discernment is not necessarily easy, but it can go a long way in opening one's eyes to the true intents of another person. The worst thing we can do is sweep their suffering under the rug or pretend the problem doesn't exist.

One of the best things we can do for them is to be patient and ask questions from the body of Christ. When we cannot, He can, so let Him.

Romans 12: 9-21: "Love must be sincere. Hate what is evil; cling to what is good. Be devoted to one another in love. Honor one another above yourselves. Never be lacking in zeal, but keep your spiritual fervor, serving the Lord. Be joyful in hope, patient in affliction, faithful in prayer. Share with the Lord's people who are in need. Practice hospitality. Bless those who persecute you; bless and do not curse. Rejoice with those who rejoice; mourn with those who mourn. Live in harmony with one another. Do not be proud, but be willing to associate with people of low position. Do not be conceited. Do not repay anyone evil for evil. Be careful to do what is right in the eyes of everyone. If it is possible, as far as it depends on you, live at peace with everyone. Do not take revenge, my dear friends, but leave room for God's wrath, for it is written: 'It is mine to avenge; I will repay,' says the Lord. On the contrary: "If your enemy is hungry, feed him; if he is thirsty, give him something to drink. In doing this, you will heap burning coals on his head.' Do not be overcome by evil, but overcome evil with good."

In my experience, one cannot fully recover without faith in God.

The five stages of recovery are, in a sense, a reversal of what happens when people become addicts. First, they physically become addicted. Then they become mentally obsessed with whatever is dominating their life. This is followed by an emotional attachment to the high one gets from the addiction. The inevitable result of this path is spiritual bankruptcy.

Whatever faith a person had takes a back-seat to the addiction. This is true of all addictions, be they drugs, alcohol, sex, gambling, etc.

Addictions inevitably lead to dangerous risk-taking, such as sexual promiscuity, driving under the influence, or taking a small powerboat into hazardous seas.

How should we, as the body of Christ, respond? I feel our policy should be to dispense grace and show through our actions how compassionately Jesus treated the broken. We should assure them of God's love and forgiveness. What we should not do is show them more guilt, shame, and judgment. We need to build bridges, not burn them.

At the same time, we need to set clear boundaries. We don't give a using addict more money or let them manipulate or mistreat us in any way. But if they are seeking help, then we should seek union with them.

Christ will set anyone free of any addiction or life-dominating sin.

Treatment is big business now, and their focus is the bottom line. They aren't cheap. When I got clean in 2004, it was at ABHS in Spokane. Many such centers are built for warehousing addicts.

There are more and more faith-based treatment centers and housing. If I were involved in treatment today, I would seek faith-based, which has a long-term focus.

There is a lot of Christian-bashing in our society today, which is destructive and counter-productive. There is a distinct line between criticizing churches for their inaction and indifference towards addicts, and bashing Christianity out of anger, despair, or ignorance. I try to remember that hurt people tend to hurt other people. When people attack Christianity, it can also be a cry for help.

Often the road to recovery is arduous. It indeed was for me. I had many months of pain, especially in early recovery. Yet, God never abandoned me in my hour of need. He was there waiting for me, and he is there waiting for you if you want.

God weeps over us, His children. He wants us to run back to Him so we may one day love and laugh with Him again.

Faith in God means believing in advance what will only make sense in hindsight. I never understood that most of my life. I get it now. Jesus himself gravitated towards those whom others rejected.

I have seen many addicts and alcoholics die from their life-dominating sin and poor choices, as well as the disease of addiction.

The 12-Steps of recovery have all brought me closer to God. I have also seen a lot of non-believing people have a problem with God. I have seen people be mad at God for many reasons, often for something that happened to them during their childhood. The reality is that if you let your rejection of God derail your recovery, drugs and alcohol will welcome you back with open arms.

Psalm 14: 1-5: "Foolish people say in their hearts, 'There is no God.' They do all kinds of horrible and evil things. No one does anything good. The Lord looks down from heaven on all people. He wants to see if there are any who understand. He wants to see if there are any who trust in God. All of them have turned away. They have all become evil. No one does anything good, no one at all. Do all these people who do evil know nothing? They eat up my people as if they were eating bread. They never call out to the Lord. But just look at them!

They are filled with terror because God is among those who do right."

Joshua 24:15: But suppose you don't want to serve him. Then choose for yourselves right now whom you will serve. You can choose the gods your people served east of the Euphrates River. Or you can serve the gods of the Amorites. After all, you are living in their land. But as for me and my family, we will serve the Lord."

The Church should be setting the standard when it comes to helping the broken.

Matthew 22:35-40: "One of them was an authority on the law. So he tested Jesus with a question. 'Teacher," he asked, "which is the most important commandment in the Law?' Jesus replied, 'Love the Lord your God with all your heart and with all your soul. Love Him with all your mind.' This is the first and most important commandment. And the second is like it. 'Love your neighbor as you love yourself. Everything that is written in the Law and the Prophets is based on these two commandments.'"

God has always been faithful. He was there even during my most difficult trials and my greatest hardships.

On the other hand, the church has been inconsistent. Once, when I had been clean for about five years, I attended a bible study at a local church. The congregation was older and more affluent. When they asked me to tell my story, I told them I was a recovering drug addict.

Their reaction was akin to as if I had just confessed to murdering a child. Their words and body language showed revulsion and fear. The women clutched their purses, and several people scowled in a way that clearly showed their disdain for me and that I didn't belong there. It felt incredibly awkward. It was also revealing. They could talk the talk of Jesus, but the idea of walking His walk was threatening to them.

James 1:2-4: "My brothers and sisters, you will face all kinds of trouble. When you do, think of it as pure joy. Your faith will be tested. You know that when this happens it will produce in you the strength to continue. And you must allow this strength to finish its work. Then you will be all you should be. You will have everything you need."

God never wastes anything, not even our heartaches and most challenging trials, as hard as they may be when we go through them. They always have a bigger purpose for God's eternal plans. And more times than not, that purpose is to help us.

God uses the improbable to do the impossible. Do you think you have what it takes? You don't. But neither do I, and neither did Moses, Joseph, Rahab, Samson, Mary, Paul, and many others who God used time and time again in the Bible. God repeatedly uses the bruised and broken.

The Church needs a wake-up call. When we mistreat the broken, it breeds anger, resentment, bitterness, pain, and suffering.

Most people spend their lives running from the Church, not toward it. It is time to break that stigma!

Typically, when you ask someone how they are, they respond, "fine" or "good". Yet, we all know that many of us are not fine or good at all. We need to see beyond these superficial answers and ask ourselves if the person is genuinely okay.

People who are broken need to know they are valued. Part of this is hearing them, acknowledging that their lived experience of suffering is real, and pray for them. Importantly, we also need to reach out to them. We can get them the help they need by referring them to the services that are available in our communities. And this goes for their families as well.

Hosea 6:1-2: "The people say, 'Come. Let us return to the Lord. He has torn us to pieces. But he will heal us. He has wounded us. But he'll bandage our wounds. After two days he will give us new life. On the third day he'll make us like new again. Then we will enjoy His blessing.'"

The Lord is the healer of all people, not just the well. He came for the broken. The church should embrace this approach as well.

Matthew 7:7: "Ask, and it will be given to you. Search, and you will find. Knock, and the door will be opened to you."

By finding a church family like I currently have at Northwest Baptist Church in Bellingham, one finds that the Church has the potential to be a bringer of hope, healing, love, acceptance, and forgiveness. They do this by building bridges with the broken rather than judging them. The Church embraces the process people need to go through for restoration and recovery. This church is a living example of what the body of Christ is capable of and stands in sharp contrast to the treatment I received from churches when I was in my youth.

I recently watched members of our congregation rally around a young man who had just gotten out of jail. They gave him big hugs and showed a nonjudgmental love that was both welcoming and healing. The young man raised his hands and worshipped Christ, and it was good.

Matthew 25:35-40: "'I was hungry. And you gave me something to eat. I was thirsty. And you gave me something to drink. I was a stranger. And you invited me in. I needed clothes. And you gave them to me. I was sick. And you took care of me. I was in prison. And you came to visit me.' Then the people who have done what is right will answer him. 'Lord,' they will ask, 'when did we see you hungry and feed you? When did we see you thirsty and give you something to drink? When did we see you as a stranger and invite you in? When did we see you needing clothes and gave them to you?39 When did we see you sick or in prison and go to visit you?' The King will reply, 'What I'm about to tell you is true. Anything you did for one of the least important of these brothers and sisters of mine, you did for me.'"

If you are feeling hopeless and broken, know that we love you. We know it hurts right now, but this will pass. Never lose heart, and don't give up. Keep knocking, asking, and seeking.

If this is where you are right now, (1) ask Jesus into your heart, (2) talk to your pastor or someone you trust, and (3) don't give up.

If you don't know Jesus, stop right now and ask him into your heart. You can say, "Jesus, I know that I am a sinner. I know that you love me and want to save me. Jesus, I know that you are the Son of God who died on the cross for my sins. I believe God raised you from the dead. I repent of my sins and, by faith, receive you as my Lord and Savior. Come into my heart, and by the power of the Holy Spirit, forgive my sins."

You will one day look back at this time and give thanks. When one has had enough and finally makes up their mind and heart to get better with God's help, all things are possible.

Romans 10:9: "Say with your mouth, 'Jesus is Lord.' Believe in your heart that God raised Him from the dead. Then you will be saved."

The first step to any problem is admitting you have one.

A prayer for the broken and addicted: "Dear Lord, I acknowledge that I am powerless over my sin and addiction. I admit that my life has been unmanageable. Even though I have tried to control it, I cannot. Please help me right here, right now. Today I understand the true meaning of being powerless. Remove from me all denial of addiction and life-dominating sin. It's in your name I pray. Amen."

If you just asked Jesus into your heart, congratulations! Welcome to the family of God. Find a Bible and a church, and get involved.

Demons are real, and I have experienced one. There is a treatment hospital where I used to be a client. I also worked there for a while. The place always had a creepy vibe to it. It was eventually abandoned, and one time my girlfriend and I returned to visit. The doors and windows were boarded up with plywood, so we removed one of the boards from a doorway to enter. We were hit by a rush of air that was probably 20 degrees Fahrenheit colder than the air outside.

We spent some time exploring, with chills running down our spines the whole time. We had entered a wing of the hospital where they had done surgeries, and the stainless-steel tables were still in some of the rooms. The corridors were long and dark.

Suddenly, my girlfriend screamed. I looked in her direction and clearly saw the shape of an eerie-looking creature with the most evil-looking eyes I had ever seen. There is no doubt in my mind that what we saw was a small demon. We also heard screaming, doors opening and closing, and footsteps running. I have never been so terrified in my life. The fiery red eyes followed us the whole time we were there, circling and watching our every move. We couldn't get out of that place fast enough. The screaming and door-slamming continued until we left. Neither my girlfriend nor I had ever been so scared as we were that night. There is no doubt our guardian angels were watching over us.

And it didn't end there. The demon followed us home that night. For several months after we visited the treatment hospital, I sometimes saw it in my hallway. And the memories of the screams and slamming doors echoed in my mind long after the sightings ceased. Satan can shape-shift. He can masquerade as an angel or a demon. I have experienced Satan's incarnations on several occasions, but this encounter surpassed them all. If you have ever had a close encounter with pure evil, you will understand what we experienced.

In **John 10:10**, Jesus says, " A thief comes only to steal and kill and destroy. I have come so they may have life. I want them to have it in the fullest possible way."

Amazingly, a few months later, I became a patient at a different treatment center next door to the abandoned one where we first encountered the demon. A few weeks after settling in, the center went into lockdown around four o'clock in the morning. As I lay in my bed, I was physically attacked. Hands closed in on my neck and tried to choke me. I fought back with all my strength against the being that was trying to kill me. It was no human, or if it was, it was some sort of grotesque incarnation of one. I can only describe it as evil and overbearing.

When I finally freed myself, I ran outside my room and found the night security guard in his office. When I entered, he was watching the closed-circuit camera that focused on the sidewalk outside the window of my room. Together, we watched in fascination and horror as a creature moved back and forth along the sidewalk. Its form was hard to make out, but it definitely had a heavy, dark presence and appearance.

Every hair on my body stood up. It was absolutely terrifying.

There is no doubt in my mind that this evil creature was trying to kill me, and that, again, my guardian angel or angels intervened to save my life.

For the next few days, my eyes had difficulty focusing. I felt like a dump truck had run over me. It felt worse than my most sickening hangover, which is saying a lot for someone who lived so long as an alcoholic.

In light of events like this, it's helpful to remember that our suffering in this life is not comparable to the Glory that will be revealed to us.

Romans 8:18: "What we are suffering now is nothing compared with our future glory."

Another time, guardian angels came to my rescue; this happened in the mid-1990s. I was working, cleaning restaurants after-hours. Once, when I finished a job around 3:00 AM, I had an ear infection, and it was pretty painful. I didn't want to go to the hospital, so instead, I took three oxycontin 80s, which is powerful pain medicine. I chewed all three of them at once, which is enough to kill some people.

I drove home in my small Geo Metro car, the long way. The road had some sharp turns, and as I approached one of them, the medicine hit me hard all at once. The car went off a ravine and flew into the air. Suddenly, the vehicle was mysteriously "put" back on the road. Had I gone over the ravine, it surely would have crushed my small car and killed me.

Nothing happens by mistake in God's world.

Luke 5:31-32: "Jesus answered them, 'Healthy people don't need a doctor. Sick people do. I have not come to get those who think they are right with God to follow me. I have come to get sinners to turn away from their sins.'"

Another time my girlfriend and I went to the hospital to get our abscesses drained. We both had them. My girlfriend and I had taken quite a bit of methadone that day. After draining the abcesses, the doctor gave us both Ativan. The hospital released us, and we stumbled out to my car. We were completely out of it. They should never have let us drive home. Suddenly, this guy just appeared in our back seat – literally out of thin air. We were alone together one second, and the next there was a stranger in the car! As we drove home, I ended up going down the wrong side of the freeway. Cars were ripping around us, many of which honked. Several times, we came close to colliding head-on with oncoming vehicles.

I managed to get the car off the road at one of the exits and stopped at a nearby McDonald's. I went inside to buy some food, and when I returned to the car the man had vanished.

Hebrews 13:2: "Don't forget to welcome outsiders. By doing that, some people have welcomed angels without knowing it."

I have lost count of the number of divine interventions that have saved my life. Unfortunately, many of my addict friends have not been so fortunate. Many have died at young ages.

My friend Tristan and I were driving down a two-lane road at about 50 mph as a dump truck approached us from the other direction. As it passed, a large brick flew out of the back of the truck and crashed into our windshield, bounced off, and flew over the top of my car. Given the size of the brick and the velocity of our two vehicles, it should have smashed right through the glass. It barely left a nick.

I stopped the car, and Tristan and I went over to inspect the brick, which had landed quite far from the site of impact. We estimated that it traveled about 200 feet and weighed over 25 pounds!

Whether it's drug overdoses, demons, or flying bricks, God's angels have been there for me.

In 2008, I had been clean for four years and moved to Redmond, Oregon, to be near my daughter, son-in-law, and first granddaughter.

I recall being in an AA meeting and asking God where I should attend church. He clearly answered to go to the one that was across the street. I didn't listen at first, but after asking and getting the same response three more times, I did as he asked.

Attending that church, Redmond Christian Church, was one of the best things I ever did. I met some of the most amazing and inspiring people there. Notable among them are my good friends, Myron and Donna Wells. Myron was the pastor at the time but has since moved on. He was instrumental in getting me to stop smoking cigarettes in 2009. That likely extended my life and saved me a fortune! I once calculated that the decision saved me over $20,000! If you smoke, please stop.

I was baptized at the Redmond Christian Church. They provided a stellar example of how a church should function. When I first entered the church as a complete stranger, they showed me unconditional love. I am truly a better man for having attended that church and having met Myron and Donna. Among many other things, they taught me accountability and provided living examples of empathy, compassion, and love. If you two are reading these words, thank you, my friends, for all you have done!

Chapter 9
Hope and Faith

**"Find your delight in the Lord. Then he will give
you everything your heart really wants."
Psalm 37:4**

No one creates a legacy by standing still.

Hope is a desire for a specific thing to happen. It encompasses
our dreams and aspirations.

Faith is a belief in a greater power. It is rooted in a spiritual
understanding and connection rather than subjective proof.

I grew up in the Lutheran Church. My mother and the
Lutheran faith instilled the morals and values I have always
held dear, even when I strayed far from God and the teachings
of Jesus.

I began to lose my way as a teenager. Like a snake shedding
its skin, I discarded many of the morals and values I had been
taught. Sin lures you in. At first, a sin is a conscious choice,
but then it becomes your lifestyle. The devil lurks like a lion
in the bush, waiting for its opportunity to pounce. It attacks
when you are weak, vulnerable, insecure, and rebellious. I
was devoured by sin and addiction, but even in my darkest
moments, I held on to those morals and values, sometimes
tenuously.

Even as addiction held me tight, I held even tighter to those
values. Even the taking of the Lord's name in vain has always
bothered me.

I worked the 12 steps throughout my early recovery which brought me closer to God. Later in my recovery, I began attending The Most Excellent Way, a Bible based ministry for people who want help from any form of addiction. I found that the Ten Attitudes of Victorious Living gave me the solution to my addiction by helping me become more God-dependent and brought me even closer to God.

The Most Excellent Way:
The Ten Attitudes of Victorious Living

When we finally get clean and sober, we must learn to live a new life with a new character. When we become new creations in Christ, we must put on His spiritual life and put off the old, worldly, prideful, selfish, lustful nature. In His Sermon on the Mount (Matthew 5, 6 and 7), Jesus describes the attitudes of His followers. "The Most Excellent Way" ministry is centered on God's Word, and Christ's Beatitudes are our foundation for change.

"Let this mind be in you which was also in Christ Jesus."
Philippians 2:5 NKJV

1 ... Humility

I admit I am powerless over the affects of drugs and alcohol, and self-centered behavior — my life is unmanageable.

Jesus said: "Blessed are the poor in spirit, for theirs is the kingdom of heaven."
Matthew 5:3 NKJV

2 ... Repentance

I believe Jesus Christ can and will create in me a new way of life.

Jesus said: "Blessed are those who mourn, for they shall be comforted."
Matthew 5:4 NKJV

3 ... Submissiveness

I give my will and my life to Jesus Christ.

Jesus said: "Blessed are the meek, for they shall inherit the earth."
Matthew 5:5 NKJV

4 ... Honesty

I honestly examine myself in the light of God's Word.

Jesus said: "Blessed are those who hunger and thirst for righteousness, for they shall be filled."
Matthew 5:6 NKJV

5 ... Mercy

I humbly ask God's forgiveness for my sinful past. I am able to forgive those who have hurt me.

Jesus said: "Blessed are the merciful, for they shall obtain mercy."
Matthew 5:7 NKJV

6 ... Obedience

I desire to live under the guidance of God's Holy Spirit — day by day.

Jesus said: "Blessed are the pure in heart, for they shall see God."
Matthew 5:8 NKJV

7 ... Reconciliation

I ask forgiveness from God and those I have hurt or dealt with unfairly.

Jesus said: "Blessed are the peacemakers, for they shall be called sons of God."
Matthew 5:9 NKJV

8 ... Faith

I trust in the power of Jesus Christ when I face hardship and trials.

Jesus said: "Blessed are those who are persecuted for righteousness' sake, for theirs is the kingdom of heaven."
Matthew 5:10 NKJV

9 ... Perseverance

I stand firm in my faith that Jesus is in control of all things.

Jesus said: "Blessed are you when they revile and persecute you, and say all kinds of evil against you falsely for My sake.

Rejoice and be exceedingly glad, for great is your reward in heaven, for so they persecuted the prophets who were before you."
Matthew 5:11-12 NKJV

10 ... Loving Servant

As a new creation in Christ, I share with others the Good News of a risen Savior who makes His people whole.

Jesus said: "You are the salt of the earth; ...You are the light of the world. Let your light so shine before men, that they may see your good works and glorify your Father in heaven."
Matthew 5:13-16 NKJV

(Used with permission.)

An unhealthy person finds fault in almost everything that others do. A healthy person understands that the actions of others have nothing to do with oneself.

Hebrews 11:1: "Faith is being sure of what we hope for. It is being sure of what we do not see."

Hope is the evidence and substance of things hoped for and not yet seen. In early recovery, I held very little hope. This was mostly because drug withdrawal is a physically and emotionally brutal process. Even in the depths of despair, I knew in my heart that, with even a tiny amount of hope, Jesus was the only answer to my pain and anguish.

Romans 8:18: "What we are suffering now is nothing compared with our future glory."

I can never compare my suffering to what Jesus felt. The pain, suffering, and death that He endured atoning for all the sins of humankind have no earthly comparison. His agony on the cross was in service to the highest and noblest of goals.

I take comfort in knowing that one day sickness and suffering will be a thing of the past. I therefore continue to live by hope and faith. Walking with Christ is not a magic formula for removing our pain and suffering. He fills our lived experience with meaning and absorbs our anguish into His own. What this boils down to is that we don't have to fight alone. God wants to send His angels to help us.

Psalm 91:11: "The Lord will command His angels to take good care of you."

In many ways, our society has programmed us to reject the Truth about our Heavenly Father and Jesus. If we had an inkling of how much we are loved, our hearts would burst.

Regarding love: **1 Corinthians 13:7-8**: "It always protects. It always trusts. It always hopes. It never gives up. Love never fails. But prophecy will pass away. Speaking in languages that had not been known before will end. And knowledge will pass away."

I do not know what tomorrow may bring, but by living in the moment, come good or bad, I know these things shall pass and hope shall prevail.

God has given me self-worth, love, and beauty out of the ashes of my broken life. My dreams were lost, and my sorrows were many. Now I have peace and my best friend, my Lord and Savior Jesus Christ, at my side.

Romans 15:13: "May the God who gives hope fill you with great joy. May you have perfect peace as you trust in Him. May the power of the Holy Spirit fill you with hope."

Hope and faith in my life today leave me in a state of love, acceptance, and forgiveness. I love myself as a child of God, and by keeping the faith, I can have the limitless strength provided for me through my daily prayer and guidance. Every day I renew my faith in Christ. He has helped me become clean and will keep me clean for tomorrow. Daily I continue my surrender to God and pray for my knowledge, hope, and faith to be strengthened.

Philippians 4:13: "I can do all this by the power of Christ. He gives me strength."

Psalm 119:92-93: "If I had not taken delight in your law, I would have died because of my suffering. I will never forget your rules. You have kept me alive, because I obey them."

Psalm 37:4: "Find your delight in the Lord. Then he will give you everything your heart really wants."

Deuteronomy. 28:1-7: "Make sure you obey the Lord your God completely. Be careful to obey all His commands. I'm giving them to you today. If you do these things, the Lord will honor you more than all the other nations on Earth. If you obey the Lord your God, here are the blessings that will come to you and remain with you. You will be blessed in the cities. You will be blessed out in the country. Your children will be blessed. Your crops will be blessed. The young animals among your livestock will be blessed. That includes your calves and lambs. Your baskets and bread pans will be blessed. You will be blessed no matter where you go."

Many years ago, my son, Loren Jr., said to me that a person just has to grow up at some point. Those were some wise words from an incredible young man. For most of my life, I avoided growing up. I did not develop the life skills to live a happy, productive life. I had little respect for other people, including myself. My focus was on feeding my destructive, drug-addicted lifestyle. The reality is that had I not grown up, that lifestyle would have dealt me an early death.

Once I recommitted my life to Christ, my life came back together.

Because of my addictions and harmful lifestyle choices, my two children, Loren Jr. and Tangela, set clear boundaries with me. They had become wise to my lying, manipulative and destructive ways and learned to protect themselves from me.

Tangela told me she would not talk to me until I had completed a full year clean. She maintained that promise. Tangela gave birth to my first grandchild in 2006. She and her husband live in Tucson.

At the time, Loren Jr. and I were not in contact. It took him a little longer than it did Tangela to accept that I had indeed changed, but he eventually saw that I had left my old ways behind. Today we have a healthy, loving father-son relationship that brings me great joy and fulfillment.

When my first grandchild turned one-year-old in March 2007, my son-in-law decided to throw a party and bought a keg of beer to celebrate. To say the least, I was not happy with his choice. They held the party at his mother's house in Phoenix. It was a strange feeling to be the only sober person at a family get-together. I was able to stay sober and connected by using my Christian faith and the tools I learned in recovery.

I cannot reclaim the years I lost with my children, nor can I undo the damage I did to them. But with God's mercy, I have been able to make amends and restore my relationships with my children and family.

There is true power and beauty in forgiveness. I now enjoy wonderful relationships with my partner, children, and grandchildren. My life today is a flower growing out of the ashes of a broken life. Every day is a gift from God.

Phillippians 4:13: "I can do all this through Him who gives me strength."

After three years clean, my life felt stable for the first time since my childhood. Early in recovery, I learned that laughter and a happy heart are good medicine.

Addiction is not necessarily inherited. My parents and children were not addicts or alcoholics.

My partner, Teresa, is my best friend and the love of my life. Together, we have four beautiful kids, four loving grandchildren, and one (Willow) who is in heaven. By the Grace of God, they will never see either of us high on drugs.

All the bridges I burned have been restored. I continue to tell others the good news of the Savior that makes His people whole. He has given me beauty for ashes.

Truly, out of the ashes of a broken life, I am a new creation in Christ

2 Corinthians 5:17: "Therefore, if anyone is in Christ, the new creation has come. The old has gone, the new is here!"

Phillippians 1:3: "I thank my God every time I remember you."

I'm thankful to be alive, especially since most of my childhood friends and those with whom I did drugs and alcohol died many years ago. I am grateful to God and His wisdom for carrying me all the years of my life. God is good. I want to thank again all my family and friends who never gave up on me. And thank you to the many people I have met in recovery.

A most special thanks to my lovely partner and best friend –
I love you more than you will ever know. And thank you all
lovingly in Him.

If you, dear reader, are tired of living a life of addiction, I
plead with you to give your life to Christ, go into recovery, get
clean, and stay clean.

To you and all the readers of this book, may the Lord bless
you and keep you.

Hymnal: "If life be long, I will be glad", by J. G. Bonnel:

If life be long, I will be glad

That I may long obey;

If short, then why should I be sad

To soar to endless day?

This life is giv'n me to prepare

For that which is to come;

Grant me, O Lord, the bliss to share

Of an eternal home.

Connecting with us:

If you would like assistance with starting a faith-based recovery group or would like us to speak at your church, please contact us at:

mcwilliamsloren@gmail.com

Appendix

Affirmations

These affirmations have either helped me in recovery or somehow touched my life in a meaningful way:

1. The three C's: Challenges, Choices, and Consequences. Our challenges lead to choices (good or bad), while our choices lead to consequences (positive or negative).

2. Before I could be brought out of the ashes, first, I had to fall into the fire.

3. Drugs and alcohol are destructive. Obsessive and compulsive behaviors led me to a type of living where I was left with only ashes.

4. We learn far more from our failures than our successes.

5. I'm not responsible for filling your cup. I am responsible for emptying mine.

6. The value of my life is always measured by how much of it I give away.

7. More than enough are His words.

8. God, when I'm at the end of my rope, give me more rope.

9. Faith is not a leap into darkness but a step into the light.

10. I am willing to take risks to become happier today.

11. Happiness is obedience; obedience is happiness.

12. If you don't have God, then you will put something else in His place.

13. Remorse is being sorry. Repentance is being sorry enough to stop.

14. Proverbs 4:23: "Above all else, guard your heart, for everything you do flows from it."

15. Grace covers our responses, so they are redemptive, not regretful.

16. Humility opens my heart to receive His grace.

17. Psams14:2: "The Lord looks down from heaven on all mankind to see if there are any who understand, any who seek God."

18. Grace says we can when circumstances say we can't.

19. Lord, please grow my heart in grace so I can give more grace to others.

20. He is no fool to give up what he cannot keep, to gain what he cannot lose.

21. Remember, if you lose time, you will never find it.

22. I will go anywhere as long as it's forward.

23. Romans 8:31: "If God is for us, who can be against us?"

24. Prayers, hugs, and love are just a few of God's blessings.

25. When it became harder to suffer than to change, by the Grace of God, I changed.

26. Focus your energy on changing yourself, not your circumstances.

27. No man is ever the same after God has touched him.

28. Be a rainbow in another person's cloud.

29. The enemy's demonic purpose is for torment, but God's divine purpose is for my refinement.

30. An unhealthy person finds something wrong with pretty much everything other people do. A healthy person understands that the actions of others has nothing to do with them.

31. John 10:10: "The thief comes only to steal and kill and destroy; I have come that they may have life, and have it to the full."

32. God moves in mysterious ways; His wonders to perform; He plants His footsteps in the sea as He rides upon the storm.

33. The Light of the world knows no power failure.

34. Hardships and brokenness are meant to grow us closer to others and, most importantly, to God.

35. We celebrate our God-given life when we show our gratitude for all of God's blessings.

36. I live my life in such a way that when others think of integrity, they think of me.

37. The question is not "Where is God?" It is "Where isn't God?"

38. Our lives mirror our relationships.

39. If you have been given a life of misfortune or handicap and yet, despite that, you have chosen to live by purpose, faith, and peace of mind, then you have succeeded where most people have failed.

40. Without God, man cannot. Without man, God will not.

41. The best, most beautiful things in the world cannot be seen or even be touched; they must be felt by the heart.

42. Pray as if everything depended on God, but work as if everything depends on you.

43. My body should be a billboard for God.

44. My flesh gambled by doing wrong and trying to get away with poor choices.

45. Lord, help me make prayerful deadlines so I can become a better steward of my time, treasures, and talents.

46. To hear sound advice and not follow it is like not even hearing it at all.

47. It's hard to stay obedient and productive while you're in pain, so trust the process of faith and surrender.

48. I do not ever want to forget how much God has blessed me and that everyone and everything I have are gifts from Him.

49. God puts people in our path on purpose each day so we can be a blessing to them.

50. Each and every day, I ask God to show me his assignments.

51. Always face the "Son" and you will never see the shadows.

52. As children of God, we always stand strong when we don't stand alone.

53. I can live in vision, or I can live in circumstance. I'm going to choose vision.

54. Satan's target is your mind, and his weapons are lies. So fill your mind with the word of God.

55. Even trials and challenges cannot blow down a person who is grounded by God.

56. Healthy relationships are the currency God blesses.

57. The hands of the diligent rule.

58. Christ has called me to step up and lead, then to step down to serve.

59. Even though I tried repeatedly, I could not outwit my addiction. I could not out-play it either. I did not stop on my own; I had to have God's divine intervention.

60. Joshua 24:1: "But as for me and my household, we will serve the Lord."

61. With God, people always have the best of things in the worst of times.

62. The Angel of the Lord gives me wisdom and courage to erect guardrails around my life.

63. Bad news is no news at all.

64. The grace of God transcends all my feeble efforts to describe it. I cannot pour it in any receptacle or container without it running over.

65. Those that God uses most effectively have been tried in the furnace of trials and heartaches.

66. God is not my undertaker; he is my gardener - He prunes the branches and weeds in my life that do not bring Him glory.

67. God cannot use a man greatly until He deeply breaks him.

68. It is my God who has enabled me to take the steps of testing and refinement.

69. All the glory goes to God, but the honor goes to those I've met on this journey.

70. Life is short, but our God is big.

71. Whatever the challenge before me, I can, and I have overcome by my God's mighty hand.

72. People may forget what you said, but they will never forget how you made them feel.

73. To whom much is given, much will be required.

74. It takes an enormous amount of energy to go through a betrayal. It takes the same amount to forgive.

75. When you feel the weakest, then you truly are the strongest.

76. Great leaders wake up in the morning and ask themselves, "What can I do today to glorify God?"

77. God created us because he loves us; He doesn't want us to be bankrupt spiritually, emotionally, and mentally.

78. Courage under pressure creates creativity.

79. Faith always precedes risks.

80. We were created by God for a greater purpose.

81. Some things will be left undone in the world unless you do them.

82. It is no accident that some of the most inspiring stories of faith come from those of us that the world would consider losers.

83. The satisfaction I had always been looking for was never found in self-gratification.

84. We are image-bearers of the most high God.

85. I am living in the grander vision God has for me.

86. God is always looking for someone to stand in the gap.

87. Fear is the total absence of faith.

88. People who are hurt, hurt other people.

89. People want to know someone cares, that you're willing to listen.

90. Before I was saved, I swore a lot; now, I can't talk that fast.

91. What's in your suitcase? The world needs you and all you carry.

92. There's a fantastic look in another person's eyes when you help them find their potential.

93. God can and will use you to bring others into His kingdom.

94. Lighthouses don't blow horns; they only shine.

95. There is no safer place to live than in the center of God's will.

96. The word of God is the single most important book in the entire world!

97. If someone gossips to you, then they will gossip about you.

98. I am too blessed to be depressed.

99. I can either be bitter, or I can be better. I choose to be better.

100. Remember, when you're in a valley of struggles and hardships, that this too shall pass.

101. Some people are so poor that the only thing they have is money.

102. Surround yourself with people that bring out the best in you.

103. Grace is free only because the giver Himself has paid the price.

104. A happy heart is good medicine.

105. Nature is a good nurse for tired bodies.

106. God's grace is like sunshine - Sonshine.

107. Faith is the soul's breathing-in of the divine spirit.

108. When talking to the lost, the idea is not to win an argument; it's to win this all for Jesus.

109. Don't let this sentiment turn into a judgmental attitude.

110. What we choose to do with the conflict in our life will determine the kind of growth we will experience.

111. When the way you live pleases God, even your enemies will be at peace with you.

112. Psalm 37:4: " Take delight in the Lord, and he will give you the desires of your heart."

113. God, in my life, work with me to plan with wisdom.

114. Things don't happen to me more; they happen for me.

115. If you want to know how to treat people better, start with the person in the mirror.

116. If you don't think you have what it takes, you're right. You don't. However, you are precisely the kind of person God is looking for.

117. Resentments come from looking at others. Contentment comes from looking at God.

118. Philippians 4:19: "And my God will meet all your needs according to the riches of his glory in Christ Jesus."

119. Lord, lead me with humility, vision to listen with understanding.

120. Lord, teach me to lead with excellence and to succeed in a way that truly honors you.

121. I don't always have to have a plan; sometimes, I just need to breathe, trust God and see what happens.

122. Laugh, then laugh some more. Laugh so much your body aches. Laugh some more.

123. Live as if the whole world is yours to take. Love as if your heart has never been broken.

124. I finally had to stop trying to make a better past.

125. God, use conflict in my life to draw me closer to you, as well as those different than myself.

126. I serve out of my recurring struggles, not out of a feeling of superiority.

127. I am saved by grace, grace alone, God's grace.

128. We are all cellular structures in need of our Lord and Savior, Jesus Christ.

129. Those of us who have lived longer have just made more mistakes.

130. We should not choose to remember what God has chosen to forget.

131. Grace draws me to God, so I'm able to draw others to my precious Lord and Savior, Jesus.

132. Humility is a prerequisite to receiving grace.

133. Humility has positioned itself to know others and to be known by others.

134. I walk with truth to invite others on my journey.

135. My love for God and others is flawed, but it flourishes in the little things I try to do for others.

136. I am an imperfect person whose heart has been transformed and perfected by a perfect God.

137.   Justification is not a license to sin but an incentive to obey.

138.   Many think the way to overcome sin is to say no.

139.   We must understand that we are not remodeled, sinners but re-made saints.

140.   God has a divine purpose for all of us.

141.   To say "I want" is better than to say "I owe."

142.   Worry is like a rocking chair, it will give you something to do, but it won't get you anywhere.

143.   If you hear the wrong voice, you'll make the wrong choice. If you hear the right voice, you make the right choice.

144.   God gives us the gift of time. What we do with that time is our gift back to God.

145.   You know you're living in Divine Purpose when you know you would rather not do anything else.

146.   The Bible has the answer to every single problem in life.

147.   Because I am saved by grace, I desire to live by grace. When I forgive others, I set a prisoner free - myself.

148.   Forgiven people need to be forgiving people.

149.   If I'm not willing to forgive others, I wonder whether I understand what God has done for me.

150.   Healing comes from being known and loved by God, not from dishonor and shame.

151. I am way too busy to worry.

152. It is better to have no excuse than a bad one.

153. The past is not really the past if it is still impacting the present.

154. To live with Jesus forever is the sum of all happiness.

155. The underlying cause of all trouble is fear.

156. Our lives begin to end the day we become silent about things that matter.

157. Grant me, Lord, that I may know myself, that I may know Thee.

158. Set your priorities for yourself, or someone else will set them for you.

159. The choices I make in life today will echo in eternity forever.

160. Don't let your history define your destiny.

161. God brings me to the throne of grace over and over and over again.

162. Don't take hold of that thing unless you want that thing to take hold of you.

163. Life is not about whether we will suffer. It's more about how we will respond when we do suffer.

164. Admitting when we are wrong is the beginning of learning what is right.

165. Change is always inevitable. Progress is optional.

166. Changing a person's environment doesn't change a person's heart.

167. If two people agree on everything, then one of them is not necessary.

168. Space is the first step, even when you can't see the staircase.

169. A healthy God-based self-image is vital if we are going to relate to others in a truly Christ-like way.

170. Don't let excuses ruin your life.

171. It's one thing to mark your Bible, but has your Bible marked you?

172. You earn trust a drop at a time. You lose it by the bucketful.

173. The most important things in life aren't things.

174. Live, laugh, love, learn, love God, and be happy.

175. If we could see God as he truly is, we would be more careful with the time allotted in this life.

176. God doesn't want me to be perfect, but he does want me to be honest.

177. There is no such thing as a self-made man. All of us were made by God, and He alone deserves the glory, not us.

178. God, work in my life today to plan with wisdom, guide with vision, lead with humility, listen with understanding, and work with excellence to succeed in a way that honors you and you alone.

179. My joyful generosity grows in my heart and soul as I am submitted to God.

180. When you consistently do the tasks of today in obedience, God gives you His directions for tomorrow.

181. As a new creation in Christ, I have been called to reflect on Jesus through my conduct and conversation. As long as I make this a priority, there's no telling how much of an impact I may have.

182. It is not a mystery that the change inside of me is not from myself. It's from the Holy Spirit.

183. The Holy Spirit has worked with me where I was, through the process of giving my life to Jesus Christ and the gift of recovery, to get me where I am and where I need to be.

184. Sometimes all we need is a hug.

185. God has closed doors in my life and has always opened a better one!

186. God is good, and He has always had a plan for my life.

187. Living in His will is exactly where I want to be.

188. His grace qualifies me for wholeness and holiness.

189. I will never be truly rich until I'm rich in Him.

190.   If you really want to be more social, then try spending more time outside.

191.   My Lord hung on a tree at Calvary, and that alone is what keeps me believing in a God of love.

192.   However deep the pit, God's love is deeper still.

193.   As is often the case, God uses very ordinary people to bring about his healing.

194.   To be complacent is to be unaware of danger.

195.   I can have a powerful impact simply by being the person God has called me to be.

196.   More people need my love, acceptance, and forgiveness more than they need my advice.

197.   A man who curses repeatedly is really not blessed.

198.   Our God is not just a God of chances, but of multiple chances.

199.   Don't be politically correct; just be correct.

200.   If you fight pride with pride, everyone loses. Confront it with a calm spirit. Then your witness for Christ wins. Tackle pride with fearless faith always. Stay poor in spirit by being rich in good deeds. Fear God and love people. Selflessness suffocates pride.

201.   We don't need to tell the future about our past.

202.   A word of encouragement can make the difference before giving up.

203. My weakness brings me to a place of humility that allows God to demonstrate His power in me.

204. The right way is usually the hardest.

205. I may have lost sight of God at times in my life, but He never lost sight of me.

206. Life has knocked me down at times, but faith has always lifted me up.

207. It's no one's business how you talk to God; just talk and be honest.

208. All the water in the world won't sink a ship unless it gets inside.

209. My happiness cannot be found in my circumstances. My joy is always found in Jesus.

210. At times when you do things for God, some people will spread rumors about you.

211. A discerning spirit is one that is in tune with the spirit of God.

212. Before marriage, the enemy will drive you together. After marriage, he wants to do everything to drive you apart.

213. The way of obedience is the only way of blessing.

214. No dreams are too big for God, so it's time to start dreaming. You can never out-dream God.

215. When you tell the truth, you don't have to remember anything.

216.   Don't live in "what if?" You can't change the past; just learn from the past and move on.

217.   The next time you are tempted to gossip or complain, resist that temptation with all your strength; you will never whine your way to the top.

218.   Discernment is not knowing the difference between right and wrong: It's knowing the difference between right and almost right.

219.   In your 20s, you feel like you're invincible, and nothing can harm you. In your 30s, you realize you need to grow up and that you should have grown up in your 20s. When you're in your 40s, you want to be a kid again, and oh, how you wish you were. When you get to your 50s, you begin to think, "Am I really that old?" Now, by the grace of God, when you reach your 60s, you realize if you were really going to live that long, you would have taken better care of yourself.

Made in the USA
Monee, IL
31 January 2022